THE KALEIDOSCOPE EFFECT

WHAT EMERGING GENERATIONS SEEK IN LEADERS

SCOTT CHROSTEK

The Kaleidoscope Effect:
What Emerging Generations Seek in Leaders

Copyright © 2017 by Abingdon Press

All rights reserved.

Published by Youth Ministry Partners, Abingdon Press, and Burlap.

Scripture quotations unless otherwise noted are from the New Revised Version Bible, copyright © 1989 National Council of Churches of Christ in the United States of America. Used by permission. All rights reserved worldwide. *http://nrsvbibles.org/*

Scripture quotations marked (CEV) are from the Contemporary English Version. Copyright © 1991, 1992, 1995 by American Bible Society. Used by permission.

Editor: Jack Radcliffe
Designer: Keely Moore

All Web addresses were correct and operational at the time of publication.

ISBN: 9781501844553
PACP10516504-01

17 18 19 20 21 22 23 24 25 26—10 9 8 7 6 5 4 3 2 1

MANUFACTURED IN THE UNITED STATES OF AMERICA

CONTENTS

DEDICATION

To my family at Church of the Resurrection, both at #RezDT and across all locations, I am grateful for the privilege and honor of sharing this holy adventure in ministry with you.

And to Wendy and Freddy, this book ultimately represents a shared sacrifice and effort to which I am equally humbled and privileged. I cannot imagine life without you, for you make life better and help me to be better at life. Love you.

INTRODUCTION

few set out to do the extraordinary, although most people do have a desire at least to become successful. And our working definition of success is largely rooted in comparison to the generations that have gone before us: our parents, grandparents, or in some cases, even our great-grandparents.

In Ancient Greece, a son measured his worth based upon his father, and a daughter upon her mother. This is how we have operated for generations, and this is problematic because things change. Generations change. Our situations and circumstances change because the world around us is always changing and evolving. The world our mothers and fathers inhabited is vastly different from the one we face, and the world we're facing here and now will be light-years away from the world our children and our children's children will inherit. Have you ever experienced this? Do you believe this to be true?

A few years ago, I was watching a documentary on the disappearing middle class in America. The premise of this study was to document the changing economic realities facing

Americans today in comparison with previous generations. What the producers uncovered was an extreme difference in available housing. In 1950, an average single-family home was just over 1600 square feet in size, and it consisted of two bedrooms, one bathroom, and just enough space to accommodate a family of five. This home would have listed for about $60,000. Today, the average new single-family home takes up approximately 2600 square feet, and it includes three to four bedrooms and three to four bathrooms. Not only are single-family homes bigger, but they are considerably more expensive. Today's new home costs just over $360,000. The houses our grandparents built to raise their families in aren't the same types of homes their grandchildren are buying today. However, generational changes aren't simply limited to the rising cost and size of our homes; it applies to how we communicate.

It used to be that when we wanted to communicate with someone, we would pick up a piece of paper and a pen. We'd take time to compose a message that would then be carried by the postal service over the course of several days until it made it to our intended target. Things have improved since those days. Technological advances have made communicating with others so much easier and more accessible than the days of handwritten notes. Our letters gave way to phone calls, which gave way to e-mail, which ultimately gave way to text-messaging, and now we communicate over social media apps hooked into our mobile devices. The world is operating at a point now where all of the information we need and more than we could ever possibly want is at the tips of our fingers. You can speak to anyone you want, anywhere in the world, whenever it is most convenient. You can also watch every sporting event in progress, witness every major news story as it unfolds, and be in the know about the most trivial facts simply by lifting your finger and swiping left or right. We have moved from living in a world that sings, "Hey, Mr. Postman," into a world that cries out, "Let Me Take a Selfie." Generations change as the world adapts and evolves. We've witnessed this in how generations change in their experience of faith as well.

Whereas 85% of the silent generation (born 1928–1945) call themselves Christians, just 56% of today's younger Millennials (born 1990–1996) do the same, even though the vast majority (about eight in ten) was raised in religious homes. Over the past seventy years, each successive generation has included fewer and fewer Christians, and the overwhelming majority of the Christians remaining today are over the age of 35.

According to Pew Research, Millennials (Generation Y) make up 13% of The United Methodist Church's worshipping body, with just 5% representing the group of younger Millennials (born between 1990–1996). According to a Pew Research Study, less than 11% of Millennials call themselves mainline Protestants. (Only 16% identify with Catholicism.) An interesting side note: Mainline Protestants make up about 14.7% of the American population, whereas the religiously unaffiliated (a group including atheists and agnostics) make up nearly 23% of the American population.

Of America's major faiths, mainline Protestants have the worst retention rate among Millennials, with just 37% staying in the fold. So when it comes to United Methodists or any mainline Protestant faith, we are dealing with fractions of fractions when it comes to engagement with Millennials, and for that matter, the emerging generations in general. Has this been your experience of church?

My assumption is that you have seen this regardless of where you are living or serving currently. As the church struggles to remain together as one, it would seem that the most common unifying factor shared amongst all churches is gray hair. This is what is binding us together, gray hair (or in my case, no hair). The disappearing presence of the emerging generations in churches across the country is another indicator of a generational shift, however, this shift is being accelerated by the church's unwillingness to change or adapt in order to meet these changing generations.

Each generation faces new and unique challenges involving new and unique problems, values, and norms, and our leadership challenge is to understand the unique identity of those we seek to meet, love, and serve. As church leaders, as pastors, as communities of faith charged with the mission of changing the world by making disciples of all nations from generation to generation according to the grace of Jesus Christ, we must understand the emerging world around us and the people in it. We must learn to become generational leaders. This requires imagination, vision, and a willingness to trust that God didn't make a mistake in choosing us to live out God's mission.

As a child born and raised in Detroit, I was shaped in a way that encouraged me to believe that I could do anything! I often looked up to the older members of my extended family, each of whom were successful in their automotive careers. My father, among others, encouraged me regularly, saying, *"Scott, you can do anything you set your mind to. You are smart, talented, and can literally do anything you want to do."* This was empowering, but something happened over time; he began to tack on an additional sentence to his words of encouragement. Over time he continued on to say, *". . . and because you can do anything, stay away from the automotive industry!"*

My entire family (immediate and extended) had been gainfully employed, connected, and intertwined with the automotive industry. That was our story, and it had been that way for generations. My family was extremely successful, but they, like so many others,.felt stuck in a limited, even declining industry. So, my dad (and family) encouraged me to break the mold and find a new measure of success in order to live into a different and unique future. I eventually pursued a career in investments, working for a couple investment companies over a six-year period of time, and then I heeded the call to become pastor, something that hadn't ever happened in my extended family before me.

Becoming a pastor was God's way of inviting me to do something new and unique, and something I had been specifically created for. As a young pastor, the thought of changing the world by the grace of Jesus Christ was energizing! The future was bright, new, and in some instances, uncharted. However, after spending time in seminary and working through the boards and conferences of the church, I realized that being a pastor isn't as energizing as I originally imagined it to be. Ordained ministry, and my experience of the church, shared a lot of similarities with the automotive industry or even our family systems. The church seemed to measure its success based on the structures, measures, and paradigms held by the preceding generations. When it comes to dreaming about the future and what might be possible, our church leadership or pastoral default is to model or defer to the patterns and practices of the preceding generations. This is a problem. Our denominational structures, our church models, and our general boards and agencies are too big, too slow, and out of touch with the mission field. We cannot simply continue practicing and proceeding in the same way simply because the generations before us did.

The Head and The Heart, an American indie band from Seattle (whose band members are all under the age of 35), sing a song entitled, "'All We Ever Do." It's a song that speaks to how we live from generation to generation, and the song builds to a chorus that says, "All we ever do is all we ever knew." I have found this to be true. The preferred pathway toward the future for most churches nowadays is to sing this song on repeat: "All we ever do is all we ever knew." In order to become the best version of the leader God is crafting and creating you to be, we must stop this. We mustn't repeat the patterns of the past in order to forge a way forward into the future; we must find ways to adapt and change to fit the future.

Charles Ferguson, a well-known United Methodist pastor, professor, author, and editor, was on to something back in 1983 when he wrote, "If well-organized programs, agonizingly debated resolutions, carefully crafted strategic plans, nobly inspired good intentions, and truckloads of denominational dollars could bring about the revitalization of the church and transformation of the world, we American Methodists would have accomplished it long ago!"[1]

The seismic shifts in our generational cultures have made our institutionally driven, top-down denominational strategy for leadership and transformation less likely and more costly than ever before. Long-time locked-in leadership structures from a general level have governed the church from the top down for the past several decades, and with each year has come steady decline. This cannot continue going forward, and it shouldn't because lasting change happens through authentic relationships, one person at a time. Lasting change emerges from the ground up, through pastors, church leaders, and their local communities living into the local mission field.

---

1. Charles W. Ferguson, *Organizing to Beat the Devil: Methodists and the Making of America* (Eakin Press, 1983).

Lasting changes happen on the ground, in local communities with grassroots relationships. This is Jesus' way.

Changing lives, transforming communities, and resurrecting churches by the grace of Jesus Christ never starts out at the top. It happens from the ground up. On Easter, the day of Resurrection, we don't sing, "Heaven, Come Down!" Instead, we sing, "Up from the grave, He arose!" In order to experience everlasting life, we must first experience death. In order to find hope, we must travel through despair first. In order to stand on the mountaintop, we have to trudge through the valley. New life springs forth from the ground up—one person, one church, one community at a time. What's interesting about this is that this is exactly what the emerging generations are looking for. They want to meet people; they want to make friends, build relationships and a local community. Generally speaking, they are at grassroots and one-on-one relationships. They want to start out small and grow from there, without losing touch with one another. This is what the church must try to do as well. In order to change the world, we have to start at the local church in the local community and then seek to move up from there.

One of my favorite lines describing the nature of The United Methodist Church is that the church is global in scope, but local in thrust. This means that the power to change the world is best employed at a local level. It is best employed in the local church when pastors and leaders are building relationships within the mission fields they are set in. It has nothing to do with big institutions, conferences, general boards, or agencies. Local churches have the power to change the world when their leaders take time to meet with nonreligious and nominally religious individuals who are living life outside of the church. When church leaders have the courage and boldness to do this with authenticity, the fruit of those relationships will ultimately have a transformative impact upon the global structures governing the world. When church leaders have the courage and boldness to do this with Millennials or even younger generations, they'll have the power to change the world for generations to come.

In the second chapter of Acts, after the Pentecost event where over three thousand Gentile converts joined the church, Peter took the floor of the church council at Jerusalem (the equivalent to the United Methodist's General Conference). After there had been much debate, Peter testified saying, "God gave those Gentiles the same gift that he gave us when we put our faith in the Lord Jesus Christ. So how could I have gone against God?" (Acts 11:17 CEV). By the power of the Holy Spirit, God had made no distinction between them and us.

In other words, Peter was asking, "Why would we discount the experience of others when it comes to faith?" The conversion of these Gentile people had produced a vibrant and thriving local ministry, and now the larger church body was calling it into question because it didn't look like anything they had ever known. Gentile converts? This was something that hadn't been done before. The council couldn't handle it, even though the local church could.

Moses dealt with this kind of resistance before as well. In Exodus, God's children clamored to go back to Egypt after being set free from captivity. Many wanted to go back into bondage before moving forward in a new direction. They wanted to go back to doing all they ever knew. But Moses pressed on, despite his peoples' cry. Peter, in the second chapter of Acts, pushed in the same way, encouraging the church to walk forward into the future by refocusing them on God's Great Commission to make disciples of all nations, Jew and Gentile, slave and free, man and woman, old and young. Our call (and our challenge) is to meet, invite, love, and serve the only ones who are missing from this list: the young, emerging generations.

Over my tenure serving as Lead Pastor of Resurrection Downtown, the downtown campus of The United Methodist Church of the Resurrection, I have had the privilege of experiencing some amazing moments in ministry. Our community that began in the heart of downtown Kansas City began as a handful of individuals and now numbers in the thousands, a large number of whom are between the ages of 18 and 35. I first met most of these individuals out in the broader community at coffee shops, races, walking their dogs, or playing with their kids at nearby playgrounds. I engaged people relationally daily by going to where they were, by starting conversations with people I didn't know in the hopes that I would make friends out of strangers, regardless of who they were, everywhere I traveled.

Acts 8 tells a story of an Ethiopian eunuch who was returning from the Jerusalem temple after having worshipped. The eunuch was reading from the Book of Isaiah when Philip, one of the twelve disciples, passed by the eunuch. Something prompted Philip to engage this person in conversation. Philip asked the eunuch, "Do you understand what you are reading?" The eunuch's response was, "How can I unless someone explains it to me?"

What followed is an amazing story about the power of relationship. Philip explained to the eunuch that the passage of Isaiah they were reading was actually pointed toward a guy named Jesus, the promised Son of God. The eunuch believed Philip, was enthralled with this new understanding, and his life was forever changed.

What is great about this scriptural story is that this eunuch had traveled all the way to Jerusalem in order to experience a religion that was outside of his personal worldview. The eunuch entered the temple and found a place that was focused on itself, its people, and its traditions. He found a place that was singing, "All we ever do is all we ever knew." The eunuch, even though he traveled so far to be with them in the temple, was rejected as an outsider, a misfit, as someone who couldn't possibly become a part of the temple's story for the future. The eunuch was left out and searching for answers. Fortunately, along came Philip, someone with the courage to pay attention and engage this outsider in a new and unexpected way: the life-changing power of Jesus Christ. This is our task as church leaders, but the eunuchs in our story are the ever-increasing collection of outsiders known as Millennials, members of Generation Z, anyone under the age of 35 otherwise known as the emerging generations.

- **How can we become like Philip in this effort to become the leaders the emerging generations are looking for?**

- **How can we become pastors, leaders, and churches that engage the emerging generations in ways that would invite them into an experience of the life-changing power of Jesus Christ?**

- **How can we become leaders who possess generational impact?**

I believe it begins when we have the courage to become leaders who boldly take it upon themselves to meet and engage the emerging generations both where they are and as they are. My hope is that this book will help us to develop as leaders and communities poised to connect with the emerging generations as a way of living into our mission of making disciples of all nations for the transformation of the world.

Our work toward becoming generational leaders begins by listening to and learning about **what members of the emerging generations want in a leader**. As we consider reaching out to these generations dancing around the margins of our faith, it is important to understand what Millennials and members of Generation Z are looking for in their leaders or in their communities of faith. Burlap Research reveals fifteen common traits that these generations wish to see in those that lead them. Out of those fifteen common traits, I believe there are five in particular that are the most essential.

After uncovering what emerging generations want in a leader, pastors and leaders must honestly evaluate which traits they have, which they can develop, and which ones they will never have. Our leadership solution, however, cannot be to change who we are in order to become something altogether different. We can't pretend to be something we are not. If that is our plan, then we will fail. Instead, in order to become a leader for the generations, we must simply find a way to **be as unique as they are**.

In the beginning, God forms us, shapes us, breathes life into our nostrils, and calls us good. God didn't make a mistake with you. You are enough by the grace of God, and what's more is that you have been created in a way that will reflect the image of God to the world around you. You are God's image-bearer, as unique as you are, which means you have been created with the capacity for revealing the good and beautiful God to the world around you. This is where the idea of the kaleidoscopes comes into play.

Kaleidoscopes are old boring toys, yet they're constructed in such a way as to entertain people of all ages with beautiful images composed of unique and colorful designs. Whenever someone picks up a kaleidoscope, holds it up to the light, and starts to turn the end, the beauty emerges and evolves. Kaleidoscopes capture the imagination of what is possible when we continue turning, adapting, and rotating our perspectives. No two kaleidoscopes are alike, and yet each has a capacity to reveal a beautiful thing to whomever picks it up. As we seek to become generational leaders, we must realize that we have been created in a similar fashion. We are uniquely made to be used as a gift and a tool (or in this case, a timeless toy) to reveal God's beauty to whomever we encounter. All we must learn to do is believe that God has actually called and equipped us uniquely to engage with the world around us, and in the process gain the courage to be present where people are in order to invite others to come and see the grace of Jesus Christ.

The **Kaleidoscopic leader** realizes that leading doesn't involve changing or compromising who he or she was created to be. Instead, such leaders are filled with a constant desire and willingness to make adaptive changes. In other words, they know how to keep turning and rotating their perspective and approach in order to solve problems or in order to reveal God's beautiful image to the world around them.

As we live into our mission field and seek to meet new people, we must not become something altogether different. We ought not trade in our old lives for something new. We aren't called to throw away the kaleidoscope we were given as children in order to get a newer, more hipster version of our old kaleidoscope. Instead, we should simply continue to rotate, adapt, and turn our ministerial approach until something beautiful emerges. In the church, this looks like constantly changing and adapting programs, invitations, and ideas in the hopes of reaching out and meeting new people. For leaders, this looks like doing whatever it takes, constantly tweaking and adjusting our ideas and strategies in order to accommodate the dynamic expectations of emerging generations. Kaleidoscopic leaders are willing to take risks. They also fail frequently. But throughout it all, they maintain their focus and identity through every twist and turn as being someone called and equipped to display God's image to the world around them.

Sometimes the process of meeting and inviting people to experience God's life-changing power and presence can be a process loaded with failure. Putting yourself out there in bold and courageous ways requires a certain amount of social risk and rejection. Even the leaders most successful at inviting people into an experience of God's power and presence will at times feel as though they are **square pegs living in a world of round holes**. After all, kaleidoscopes don't seem like they should stack up all that well against the technology-based toys found in today's toy stores. To this end, God reminds us in Genesis, and Jesus reinforces this in John, that God doesn't make mistakes in creating, calling, and equipping us for the mission at hand. However, becoming a generational leader will be a journey full of challenges.

Church leaders face two types of challenges: adaptive challenges and technical challenges. Kaleidoscopic leaders are leaders who have a great grasp on the power of leading through adaptive challenges. They faithfully rotate, tweak, and experiment as they scramble forward. However, all of the adapting in the world can't help overcome the technical challenges. What I call technical challenges are the physical and institutional barriers that separate us from the larger, modern world, particularly when it comes to the emerging generations. These are sometimes defined as operational problems. Kaleidoscopic leaders can define and distinguish between these two challenges, and with some simple tweaking, they can navigate the technical pitfalls that prevent Millennials from paying attention, heeding direction, and experiencing the life of Christ.

In addition to overcoming technical challenges, there are several things we can do to foster increasing connectivity with the world around us, specifically as it applies to the emerging generations. Through my B+ work at Resurrection Downtown, I've come to articulate five primary challenges to establishing and maintaining irresistible leadership environments for emerging generations. Overcoming these five challenges are essential for churches and leaders hoping to create spaces for meeting and speaking to emerging generations. Understanding the importance of hospitality, creativity, anonymity, mystery, and authenticity is critical to becoming a generational leader. Together we'll explore **the five primary facets of irresistible leadership environments** and give shape as to how you can work to create compelling environments for the emerging generations.

Finally, one of the most important disciplines necessary to becoming an effective leader for generations to come requires having the propensity for constantly **measuring your leadership effectiveness**. Today's leader must seek to find ways in which to constantly improve as a leader. Leaders must honestly evaluate their leadership effectiveness. Personally, I am horrible at this, and this has largely been rooted in asking the right questions of the right people. Lovett Weems, Director of the Lewis Center for Church Leadership, shares how the best leaders aren't the people with the right answers, but the right questions. Today's leaders must be evaluative. Constant evaluation and assessment is critical to measuring and maintaining one's leadership effectiveness.

The pertinent questions vary in their scope and audience. The first set of questions leaders should be asking are questions directed toward God through prayer. Leaders must continually ask questions of God pertaining to purpose, mission, and vision. In addition to questioning God, leaders must also ask questions of their staff, their church leaders, and anyone considered to be influential to the mission at hand. Finally, leaders must focus their questions out into the mission field in order to gain proper perspective of self-efficacy and institutional accountability.

By opening your life up to these three rounds of evaluative questions, leaders can become better equipped to thrive in mission. I'll be sure to share a framework for identifying the right questions and who I believe the right people to be in order to secure the effectiveness and legitimacy of your current leadership capacity, as well as your potential capacity within your community. Sadly, I feel that a large portion of long-time locked-in leadership would rather see the church continue to struggle than change. By asking questions and soliciting feedback, we have the opportunity to continue adapting and changing to live into the future with hope God has for us.

I believe that God has created us, called us, and equipped us to lead uniquely for such a time as this. We have everything we need in order to become the best versions of the people or leaders God created us to be. If we are willing to meet, listen, and invite the emerging generations to join us doing whatever it takes, we'll change the world.

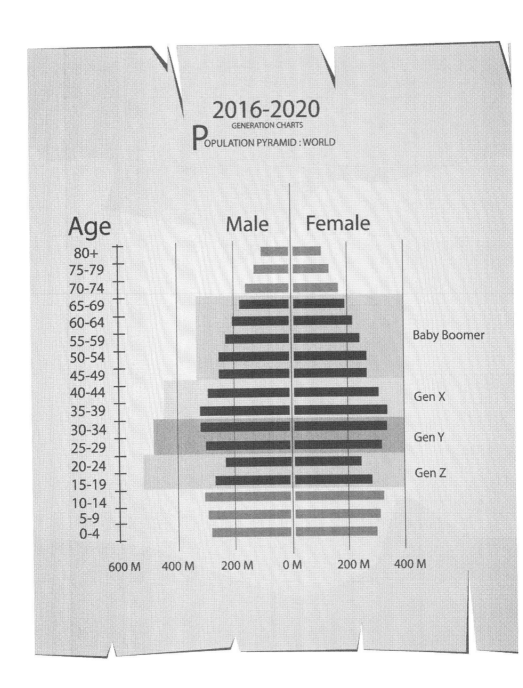

2016-2020
GENERATION CHARTS
POPULATION PYRAMID : WORLD

Age   Male   Female

Baby Boomer

Gen X

Gen Y

Gen Z

80+
75-79
70-74
65-69
60-64
55-59
50-54
45-49
40-44
35-39
30-34
25-29
20-24
15-19
10-14
5-9
0-4

600 M   400 M   200 M   0 M   200 M   400 M

CHAPTER 1

WHAT EMERGING GENERATIONS WANT IN A LEADER

I was asked a few years ago to lead a workshop describing my ministry and insights from working with a large number of people aged 18–35 at Resurrection Downtown.

The workshop had been created for a large group of pastors and leaders serving established, long-standing churches throughout the United States. In the workshop, I shared some insights that I believe to be true about the emerging generations. However, before I shared anything, I wanted to encourage the group that the best way to lead is by listening and learning in order to get to know the mission field and the people in it. I began by sharing the three questions that I heard most often from members of the emerging generations during my time in downtown Kansas City.

1) Who am I?
2) Why am I here?
3) What am I supposed to do with my life?

"100% all I think about and talk about with most of the young adults I get coffee with."

These three questions reside at the core of the emerging generations' thinking. Embedded within the younger population is a driving concern for purpose, meaning, and fulfillment. These are the substantive questions that fuel everything they do. Their answers to these questions shape their life decisions about work, school, family, friends, where they live, what they buy, and ultimately, what they choose to do with their life.

I was sitting at a restaurant not too long ago where I met up with a young professional over lunch. I thought the conversation would center on sports or pop culture. While we were making our way through our respective salads, things took an unexpected turn toward the serious. The young professional said, "Scott, the reason I invited you to lunch is because every time I see you walking through the neighborhood, I find myself longing for what you have. I wish I shared the same sense of purpose as you have."

As the lunch continued, this young man described an emptiness he always carried with him. He told me about how his life was missing something. On the outside, he was a successful individual: an accomplished professional living a very healthy life. But something was lacking. He wasn't happy or fulfilled. He didn't feel whole.

"This reminds me of the minimalist movement. A lot of my friends are talking about these two dudes and how they completely changed their life around by getting rid of what they didn't need because they weren't fulfilled." [Link– http://www.theminimalists.com.]

I have found this sense of personal longing for fulfillment to be consistently articulated by the emerging generations. I have learned this through countless conversations in coffee shops, bars, and restaurants throughout the city.

The emerging generation, as I define them, are young adults under the age 35. The emerging generations are the collection of the Millennial generation (Gen Y) in addition to the younger generation (Gen Z). These are the people who have been parented by Baby Boomers. These are people who can still remember the advent of the Internet or who grew up with cell phones and e-mail. They are also the people that experienced or remembered clearly either the Challenger explosion and/or 9/11 as being a life-shaping event. Similarly, Generation Z is a generation raised by people on the cusp between Boomer and Generation X. They can't remember a time when there weren't smartphones, when e-mail wasn't a thing, or when people had a use for VCRs (remember those?) or in some cases DVDs, only Blu-rays.

I've been in ministry with a large number of Millennials over the past several years wherein I have learned that they have been shaped with a unique worldview that carries a set of unique expectations or lack of expectations. They have no expectation of lifetime employment whatsoever. Young adults don't expect to work for the same employer over the course of their lifetimes. You might be wondering what does this have to do with the church or their life of faith. It means that this generation isn't necessarily loyal to any institution, whether it is a company, a denomination, or even a local church. The days of a lifetime Methodist, Catholic, Muslim, or Buddhist are gone in the same way that lifetime employees are rare.

At the same time, while it is not placed in institutions, I have found that there is a deep sense of loyalty that resides at the core of the emerging generations. You see this loyalty shine when there is unwavering alignment with their passion, personal mission, or values. Millennials aren't going to stay with the church unless it aligns with who they are and fulfills their needs. In those instances, the emerging generations can be fiercely loyal. Consider for a moment the brand-loyalty amongst the emerging generations with companies like Google, Toms, or Apple.

Another thing I've learned about the emerging generations is that they possess a keen sense of vision. Some people have described the emerging generation differently. They comment that the emerging generations are entitled, carry inflated self-impressions and unrealistic expectations of others, and are hesitant to do the work required to change those perceptions.

"I know people my age who won't go to church simply because they don't know what the church is passionate about. That's why churches need to state who they are instead of hoping you figure it out."

Older generations share how the emerging generations have great ideas, but no clue as to how to translate those ideas into reality. During my ministry, I've grown to appreciate the emerging generations' vision, impression, and expectations, even in the absence of physical or tangible work. The members of the emerging generations that I have encountered have been equipped to see things others cannot. They have a way of grasping the big picture when others are unable. The problem is that they do not know how to effectively make change. This doesn't make them entitled or opinionated, it makes them human.

These visionaries are in need of valued relationships with people who find life in "getting things done." The emerging generations need the influence and mentorship of the generations that have gone before. The question I pose to people of older generations is, "Are you willing to help them, join them in their vision, and collaborate to make change happen?" The emerging generations covet these types of relationships with people of varying ages, gifts, and skill sets. That's a part of the entrepreneurial spirit that sets them on fire and allows them to dive fully into their most sought-after role, which ultimately is to become their own boss.

What does this mean for the church? A church without a big vision—or any vision—for the future may be largely irrelevant to emerging generations.

I am reminded of Paul's words, "By the power at work within us, [you will be able] to accomplish abundantly far more than all we can ask or imagine" (Ephesians 3:20). This vision and imagination needs to be matched with freedom and flexibility to own, shape, and express it in both the what and how of church life and ministry. They need leaders who not only provide the opportunities, but also help them do it.

The generation you are trying to reach has grown up with instant gratification and easily explainable outcomes. My generation was a generation that had to learn the principles of long division out of necessity. When it came to math class, I had to show my work and explain my answers. The emerging generations simply hold up their calculators, tablets, or Wikipedia.

In order to meet the emerging generations where they will be, leaders must ensure that ministries or programs have tangible outcomes or impact and don't require extraordinary or superfluous training. Churches and their leaders should focus on programs and ministries that allow for drop-in opportunity and participation that demonstrates real and immediate impact, such as food drives, construction blitzes, and other serving opportunities. Additionally, churches that can figure out ways to generate big give-movements or who give away their Easter or Christmas offerings to meet direct needs will likely be able to draw attention and participation from emerging generations in ways that others cannot.

I've learned many things about this generation through my Kansas City coffee shop conversations. (I'll share those findings in Chapter 5, *Cultivating and Sustaining Irresistible Leadership Environments*.) More than anything else, though, I have learned this: The emerging generation wants to be seen and treated as unique, to be engaged right where they are, to have opportunities for immediate participation, and to have their participation translate in very relevant and tangible ways.

This is what they're craving. However, in order to ever find these things, they must have a leader they respect and trust who will galvanize them to action. To this end, I have found that the emerging generation has some very specific opinions about who that leader needs to be.

LEADERSHIP TRAITS IMPORTANT TO MILLENNIALS

In 2016, Burlap completed a survey of one hundred Millennials and asked them this question: "What are the most important traits in a leader that you would want to follow?" As you can imagine, they had a wide range of responses because of this generation's particularity, but they eventually distilled the many responses down to fifteen key traits of leaders that Millennials would want to follow.

15 Key Leadership Traits

Authenticity

"Amen. Amen. Amen."

Humility
Vulnerability
Listening
Empathy
Relatability
Vision
Passion
Communication
Spirituality
Optimism

Discipline
Determination
Team Player/Collaboration
Integrity

Following, you'll find a deeper description of each key leadership trait in order that you might evaluate and assess your own leadership competency and your church's demonstrated character and culture.

Authenticity and Humility

Authenticity refers to being genuine and real. Authenticity is more important than having authority. As one of my Millennial staff members puts it, the emerging generations have a "BS" meter that is dialed in better than most. That means that the emerging generations know when people are pretending to be something they aren't. The emerging generations are highly intelligent and can smell out "BS" whenever it is present, even in trace amounts. They long for people to be real with them. "Say it straight and make it plain." Authenticity is the highest valued of the leadership traits for Millennials.

This shared drive for authenticity, for people to be real, ultimately motivates the emerging generations to seek out leaders who communicate openly with their staff teams, communities, or congregations in a truthful, sincere, and candid manner. Authentic leaders are not concerned about being someone they are not or impressing others around them. This is evident in speech, dress, musical taste, and a variety of other things. Pastors and leaders who are trying to play it cool by saying the right things, listening to the right music, or wearing the right clothes are easily identified as playing cool as opposed to being cool. I'll never forget hearing a sermon where the preaching pastor used a lyric from a Beyoncé song—only in making the reference mispronounced Beyoncé's name, making it almost indecipherable to the listener. This is not authenticity; this is trying to be something you are not. The emerging generations can see right through this.

At Resurrection Downtown, it has been a challenge to avoid being seen as cool, simply because we are a downtown church. It's a challenge largely because we aren't cool (and we absolutely know it). However, due to our location in the heart of the city and our newness on the landscape, there is pressure to play the part. We constantly resist that temptation to be anything other than the people we are. Our informal motto has become that Resurrection Downtown is a community that longs for people to come as they are, whatever that may mean. We long for people to feel comfortable being who they are, complete with their doubts, questions, insecurities, underdeveloped fashion sense, or complete lack of hipster style. We are a church for everybody, with a staff representing everybody from retired soccer moms to young musicians, left-leaning politicos to buttoned-up CPAs. Everyone is welcome whether they're from Wall Street or simply live on the street. As a leader of this community, I make a point of leading as the person I am—uncool in the best of circumstances.

As I think about my leadership style, I would say that my title should be Lead Pastor of Awkward Encounters. I am a misfit who makes mistakes, saying the wrong things at the wrong times a good portion of the time. I am as far from perfect as they come. Ask anyone in Kansas City and they'll share with you that I am a Detroit Tigers fan who drinks entirely too much coffee, living in a city known for its Chiefs, Royals, jazz, craft beer, and barbecue. That said, I am comfortable with who I am. I believe that I am not too cool for anyone, and I don't try to be. I am comfortable in my own skin and my life experiences, both of which God has given me for better or for worse. Moreover, this comfort has allowed me to share all of my idiosyncrasies and imperfections candidly and vulnerably with those around me. This is authenticity. This is simply being real. And for the emerging generations, this is something that draws them closer because it allows them to be open in the same way. The emerging generations long for leaders who are as open as they are.

I suppose some might call this humility. At its core, authenticity is really about not thinking of yourself more highly than you ought to. In the garden of Eden, the Old Testament authors referred to this as being naked and unafraid. For Jesus, it looked like a life defined by the practice of self-emptying. Paul referred to Jesus' power as being rooted in his willingness to take the form of a servant, even though he had the power of God. Authenticity is further similar to humility in that both require an admission of shortcomings and openness to learning from everyone and every situation you encounter. Humble leaders or authentic leaders are not dominating personalities. Instead, their vulnerability is noticeable, and they appreciate the contributions of others without any jealousy or condescension.

Vulnerability and Listening
It is no surprise then that the emerging generations are looking for vulnerability within their leadership. Vulnerability is about being open to all types of feedback and questions, especially to criticism. When leaders display vulnerability by inviting feedback or asking for input, followers will see them as human, approachable, or "just like everyone else." This gives followers the confidence to share their real feelings

as well, knowing that it will be well-received and possibly make a difference. The emerging generations long to offer feedback and ideas for improvement to make whatever they are participating in better! In order to model this pattern of vulnerability at Resurrection Downtown, after every one of our Bible studies or community groups, we pass out anonymous evaluations to participants in order to learn about how we can continue to improve our effort as teachers and leaders within the church.

Another way we demonstrate that their voices matter is by inviting the congregation to share their suggestions for sermon themes and topics every summer. This input serves as a guide to plan sermon series more than eighteen months in advance. In addition to these practices, every other year we invite the entire congregation to participate in a churchwide survey that evaluates all aspects of our ministry. On that survey, we include space for specific feedback, critique, and a place for people to share their dreams for our community and our desired level of impact. If we aren't inviting constant feedback, then we are pretending as though we have it all figured out. The emerging generations are looking for leaders who are able to listen, act, and discern a way forward even amidst failure in order to continue striving for perfection, or at least improvement. However, improvement will only happen if you make yourself vulnerable and possess a willingness to listen and learn by asking others to help by sharing their thoughts, experience, and expertise.

A popular way of inviting Millennials for their input is crowdsourcing or community-sourcing. The term *crowdsourcing* was originally coined in 2006 by a group of users on social media. It describes a way of broadcasting problems to a mass audience in the hopes that they might come up with solutions. The results of an increased value on vulnerability and listening in leadership have been astounding. Just think about Wikipedia! On sites like Wikipedia or even YouTube, the pooled wisdom and expertise of the crowd has come together to create a network of solutions and creativity unlike any other.

NASA has even employed crowdsourcing as it seeks to further develop its technology without significant research costs. Science academies and natural resource managers are getting in on this resource too. Scientists are crowdsourcing "citizen scientists" that they might prevent the extinction of several rare frog species. *iNaturalist.org* launched the Global Amphibian Blitz, a citizen science–social networking drive to gather information on amphibians around the world. The website asked participants to take photos of the frogs they encountered and upload them to the *iNaturalist* site with GPS information. By being in the right place at the right time and armed with a camera, anyone can provide information that scientists could never dream of collecting on their own. The Global Amphibian Blitz launched on May 25, 2014. By the end of the first day, 154 species from eighteen countries had been photographed and geo-tagged . . . by now, they've far surpassed two thousand species of frogs.

Additionally, *Kiva.org* allows people to take the place of big banks in order to help individuals in underdeveloped countries receive micro-loans that provide opportunities for people to build new businesses. News companies crowdsource all sorts of footage for breaking news items. Crowdsourcing is changing how we live, and it is speeding up our ability to receive and process information, which means we can do things quicker and better than ever before. All of this happens only if we are willing to listen.

Empathy and Relatability

Empathy is the ability to understand and be aware of the feelings of others. Being empathetic requires a desire to understand how one's actions impact or affect the world around you. This requires great self-awareness, as well as the desire to always put the interests of others before your own.

When it comes to understanding the experience of others in conflict, conversation, and counsel, the emerging generations are looking for leaders who are attentive to cultural differences and differences in personality and strength without judgment. They won't jump to negative conclusions, but will always think the best of those around them and filter responses and actions by seeking first to understand the source of the conflict, difference, or deficiency. Leaders who take the time to understand where others are coming from, consider what others have been through and what underlies their specific motivation or behavior will draw followers from the emerging generations.

I consider empathy to be defined simply by one's willingness to walk a mile in another's shoes. Leaders don't have to understand completely, but they must possess a heart for appreciating and understanding what others have experienced in order to continue to learn from, care for, and build community with people of diverse backgrounds.

Emerging generations are also seeking relatable leaders. Relatability incorporates the capacity to empathize with others, but goes one step further. Relatable leaders must be willing to put themselves in somebody else's shoes and feel the things they feel. Being able to relate and specifically identify with others requires that leaders care about how they feel, value their experiences, and have a genuine desire to relate to them. Relatability ultimately draws people together through shared experiences, whether painful or joyous. This is also how Jesus called his disciples to live. Paul reminded the earliest Christians, saying, "Rejoice with those who rejoice, weep with those who weep. Live in harmony with one another; do not be haughty, but associate with the lowly; do not claim to be wiser than you are" (Romans 12:15-16).

The emerging generation is looking for leaders with relatablility.

Vision, Passion, and Communication
Visionary leaders encompass the capacity to imagine the possibilities of the mission or cause five to ten years down the road. Communicative leaders have the ability to communicate and compel the importance of such vision. The ability to communicate effectively is something that the emerging generations require, in that one of the most common felt needs amongst Millennials is a longing to know how "to get there."

Members of the emerging generation have grand visions of what they'd like to accomplish or become, but don't know the in-between steps. Leaders who have courage to verbalize a collective vision and communicate how to accomplish it provide a road map for the journey Millennials are seeking. Leaders who can eliminate or minimize confusion as it pertains to the "how" have the power to lead the emerging generations to the very place they long to go. At Resurrection Downtown, this has forced us to articulate how drop-in missions, weekly worship, creative hymnody, even the regular passing of the offering plates serve together to transform the heart of community we live in. This has been crucial to the fulfillment, meaning, and purpose that the emerging generations crave.

Leaders who can communicate God-sized visions alongside corresponding steps and pathways toward living into those visions are the kind of leaders anyone would follow. I think about my staff, the majority of whom are under the age of 35. When they understand how their individual job responsibilities and daily tasks (as mundane as they might seem from time to time) work together to accomplish our broader vision, their disposition, commitment, and productivity increase exponentially. The emerging generation longs to know how to get there. Make it plain for them.

Our vision at Resurrection Downtown is to transform the heart of Kansas City proper. This happens as we build Christian community where nonreligious and nominally religious people are becoming deeply committed Christians. In order to make this happen, we need to involve hundreds of volunteers each week divided into various teams. These teams each serve in very specific ways. We have one team of volunteers that spends 250 hours combined each year simply inputting attendance data from our worship services. These volunteers sit in front of their computers for 250 hours typing in the names, addresses, e-mails, and phone numbers for everyone who attends one of our worship services. Can you imagine the potential drudgery of this? This is not what most people think about when they think God is calling them to change the world. And yet for these volunteers, they are passionate and committed to this weekly practice because they know without a doubt that in keeping great attendance and contact information, they make possible the ability for hospitable follow-up.

If everyone who comes to worship received a follow-up phone call, a prayer note, or some other form of communication, then their lives could be changed or impacted in some way. The only way this can happen, the only way we can meet people where they are with loving kindness and follow-up is by keeping good data or by inputting these names. For 250 hours each year, these volunteers input data because they see how their daily practices serve to change or in some cases, quite literally, save lives.

Leaders must communicate big vision and the important steps as to how we get there *with passion or fervor.* Passion relates to the love that individuals have for their work and the determination with which they perform their duties and responsibilities. Passion is a must for leaders as it is what drives them and fuels their hunger or craving to accomplish a goal or see a vision fulfilled. Your heart has to be in it. John Wesley, the founder of the Methodist movement, would often ask his leaders, "How goes it with your soul?" He did this as a way of checking in on their faithfulness and well-being. The question a Millennial might prefer to ask their leaders is, "How goes it with your heart?" They want to know if their leaders are in love with the mission.

Spirituality and Optimism

Spiritual leaders who count their blessings are extremely grateful and are not tainted by egoism. They generously compliment people who are dedicated and hard-working, and choose to see possibilities even when others cannot, especially in the presence of problems and hurdles. They are also very approachable and encouraging, knowing that there is a larger force at work in the world. Spiritual leaders aren't swayed in the tumult of the world with swirling opinions and trends.

When I think about a capable spiritual leader, I think about someone who is always attentive to the fact that God is with us, that God's promises are true. Paul says that there is *nothing we can do that would ever separate us from the perfect love of God* (Romans 8:37-38 paraphrased). In fact, he is so bold as to say that this perfect love casts out all fear (1 John 4). The only way this can be possible is if we remember God is with us. Remembering and not forgetting requires spiritual discipline, namely, practicing the seven dimensions of a spiritual life (see *Pursuit*[2]). By this, leaders ought to maintain a posture of gratitude and service as opposed to self-directed, ego-driven leadership.

I believe that effective spiritual leaders must also be optimists or people of hope. Optimists are people who love to see the positive side of things even in the most difficult of circumstances. They are able to cling to hope even in the wake of despair. When faced with failures or hurdles, optimistic leaders take them as learning experiences and do not accept defeat for failure. Optimistic leaders' motto is to keep pressing on in the hope of things getting better in the near future. It is living a life that continues to sing: "We know that all things work together for good for those who love God, who are called according to his purpose" (Romans 8:28).

Discipline and Determination

Discipline relates to control and focus attained by way of adhering to a certain standard of rules. Leaders who are disciplined are typically calm, well-organized, and have a clear set of priorities and objectives. They have a good sense of control over their emotions and over their actions, thoughts, and speech.

---

2. Scott Chrostek, *Pursuit: Living Fully in Search of God's Presence* (Beacon Hill Press, 2012).

If you are going to keep moving forward without confusion in the midst of life's storms, you have to be determined to press on. Airline pilots and boat captains, when facing turbulence or choppy water, increase their speed to cut swiftly through the air or water in order to keep moving forward. This should be true of organizational leaders. We must be willing to do whatever it takes to keep moving forward, especially when the waters get rough. A pastor friend always told me that leaders are the ones who keep their foot on the gas pedal when everyone else wants to pump the brakes or slow down.

Our determination is best demonstrated in the focus and will of staying true to one's purpose. It is about the continuation of your hard work even in difficult times. Determination is firmly carrying through with your plans with a strong resolve, and belief that you will achieve your objective, overcoming everything in your path, even failure. Followers want to know that leaders have a "do whatever it takes" mentality.

Team Player/Collaboration and Integrity

Collaborative leaders are those who know the value of interpersonal relationships in the success of an organization, mission, or cause. When leaders are good at being team players, they accept and acknowledge their responsibilities and communicate with their team in an open and transparent manner. Collaborative leaders seek to thrive by finding others who posses different skills and abilities, and find ways to deploy them uniquely according to the gifts they've been given to their fullest expression for a common vision.

When we assembled our team of people to launch Resurrection Downtown, I had to find people who could do things and think of things that I couldn't. *StrengthsFinder* has been a great tool for sharing insight about what we are lacking as a staff team, as well as where we are each our strongest. In the same way that the apostle Paul spoke of the body of Christ with many members but one spirit (1 Corinthians 12), the emerging generations are looking for leaders who are willing to recognize the importance of contributions from a diverse community of people and participants.

After reading through this list, how are you doing? How do you feel? Do you possess all of these qualities? Half? Are there any that seem to be far removed from who you are? Regardless of how many of these traits you possess, these are the traits that the emerging generation is looking for in a leader. As we strive to bridge the gap by living into our call to make disciples of all nations, ages, and races, my hope is that you will keep these traits in mind.

You don't have to possess all of these qualities, but the more you display them, the more effective your Kaleidoscopic leadership will be.

Questions for Reflection

1. Which leadership traits best characterize your approach to or style of leadership?

2. What traits from this list are missing from your own personal approach to leadership or your church's?

3. What do you look for in a leader? How does it compare with Burlap's list of 15 Key Leadership Traits for Emerging Generations?

4. What does your community desire in a leader?

humility
GENTLENESS
patience
LOVE
-EPHESIANS 4:2-

CHAPTER 2

BE AS UNIQUE AS THEY ARE—KALEIDOSCOPE EFFECT

Understanding what Millennials are looking for is one thing, but creating irresistible leadership environments that draw them into our churches is something altogether different. Our leadership solution for overcoming this challenge cannot be as simple as attempting to change who we are as individuals, lay leaders, or pastors. We do not need to run out and buy new clothes, listen to new music, or alter the way we talk about politics or theology. Nor do we need to start a brand-new worship service or create a new webpage with a bunch of sleek, stock photographs. We must offer much more substantive change in order to succeed. We must be the unique people that God created us to be, as odd and as imperfect as that may seem.

I think one of the greatest leadership principles we can embrace when seeking to meet the emerging generations is constantly remembering that God didn't make a mistake in creating you. God formed you, shaped you, and uniquely gifted you for such a time as this. Moreover, I believe God called you into God's world-changing mission to make disciples of all nations for generations to come. This has been my experience in ministry.

A few years back, I wrote a book detailing and describing my experience of launching Resurrection Downtown, a church that now worships over a thousand a weekend. Of those thousand people, approximately half of them are under the age of 35. I'm certain a good portion of our success as a church has been the way we've attracted younger people.

But we haven't always been that way.

When we began in 2009, we had nothing more than a handful of committed individuals as diverse as they come. I refer to the early days of this adventure as *God's Misfit Mission*. In that book, I share how God had assembled a ragtag group of individuals with nothing in common (misfits) to launch a church in the heart of Kansas City. That chapter of my life was the most defining moment in my ministerial life. It was in walking up and down the streets of KC inviting people to the church that I realized for the first time that God didn't make a mistake in bringing me to the Midwest. In fact, I learned something much greater than that. I actually learned that whenever the God of the universe wants to do something extraordinary, God will always choose "the wrong people" to do it. And I was the wrong person.

God chooses us—God's imperfect, insecure, ill-equipped messengers—in order to accomplish God's mission on earth. I've come to believe firmly that misfits are God's "plan A" when it comes to changing the world to better reflect God's kingdom.

So if you find yourself under stress and wondering what in the world you are doing in a certain part of the country in a church you never imagined working for—and most likely well out of your comfort zone—relax! You are right where you are supposed to be.

In the fourteenth chapter of John, Jesus tells his disciples, "The one who believes in me will also do the works that I do and, in fact, will do greater works than these" (John 14:12). In this passage, Jesus is assuring his disciples that no matter what they may think, God created them (as imperfect and fallible as they often likely felt) with extraordinary abilities to do the same amazing, otherworldly things as God did. God makes possible things of abundance, far greater than anything we could typically dream, through us.

In his letter to the Ephesians, writing from prison, the apostle Paul urged his community to never forget their capacity for doing great things in God's name. Paul reminded his Ephesian congregation of God's immeasurable power, saying, "To him who by the power at work within us is able to accomplish abundantly far more than all we can ask or imagine" (Ephesians 3:20). In confinement, Paul was able to remind his churches that by God's grace, they had the power to change the world. It doesn't matter how stuck they were, how inadequate they felt, or how dark things may have seemed. By the power of God's grace, together they could still achieve the extraordinary. This is still the story almost two thousand years later.

God calls each and every one of us to be an integral part of God's team of misfits wherever we are located in order to live into an unimagined future full of hope. This is God's commission. Our marching orders are to simply respond with courage and confidence in faith. When we do, we begin to live differently—with God-sized vision—something that the emerging generations (if not every generation) seek. The emerging generations are drawn to leaders and congregations who are comfortable in their own skin and who believe that they are uniquely called to transform the world by doing the things that God does. They are looking for people who stand out—people who are unique; people who have big vision. They are longing to connect and do life with people and churches who break typical church molds and differentiate themselves with genuineness and authenticity.

The emerging generations are longing for authentic, empathetic leaders who are willing to listen and learn to the world around them. They see everyone in it as having something unique to share. In the same way that most Millennials might cringe at the thought of being just like everyone else, they desire leaders who treat everyone as unique, independent, and as God's singular, beautiful creation. In fact, no two Millennials are the same. We MUST treat them each as unique beings. Therefore, if we are trying to be the same as other churches, embodying the same trends, we will absolutely alienate young adults. Our leadership task is to embrace the unique identities within the emerging generations not by changing and becoming something we aren't, but by simply having the courage to be as unique as they are—as individual, independent, and as quirky as can be.

If this sounds like a tough challenge, perhaps because you were called to a church with little history of change, take heart! It doesn't matter how old you are, how small your church is, or how modern and trendy you may appear to be or not to be. The God of the universe says, "I created you!" God meant it when God invited you to a place of leadership within the church. When Jesus called his disciples, most of them were simple tradesmen. He reminded them, saying, "You did not choose me but I chose you [when you were fisherman]. And I appointed you to go and bear fruit, fruit that will last" (John 15:16).

It doesn't matter who we are or what we know how to do when the time comes. The simple fact is this: God chooses us first. God stirs a passion within our misfit hearts and then equips us with purpose and vision to build Christian community and to change lives. This is God's way. You simply have to know you are God's wonderful tool and that God didn't make a mistake with you.

Therefore, our leadership strategy to reach the emerging generations cannot be simply to change who we are in order to meet people where they are. That's important. First, we need to remember who made us and called us.

When I think about what being an effective leader for the emerging generations looks like, I cannot help but think about kaleidoscopes. I have come to understand my leadership potential as similar to that timeless toy from our childhood.

Having a toddler in the home for the very first time in my life, I have become reacquainted with these amazing toys from generations past. Kaleidoscopes are these beautiful, telescope-like toys filled with colored glass. Whenever someone holds a kaleidoscope to their eye and points it toward the light, it creates a unique collage of colored light that changes in design and beauty as the end is rotated. Each kaleidoscope is unique. The possibilities of new beauty within each kaleidoscope are infinite. From the Ancient Greek, *kaleidoscope* when translated means "to look at or see beautiful things." Kaleidoscopes are tools that are created with the sole purpose of helping the world around them to see a lifetime of beautiful things. We, as God's chosen leaders, are the same way, only our responsibility is to help the world around us to see the life-changing power of Jesus Christ.

Church leaders are better understood as kaleidoscopes made useful by the light of Christ working in and through us to reveal the good and beautiful things of God. By this light, we have the unique capacity to do the things that God does. As God's kaleidoscopes, created to reveal beautiful things to the world around us, we can change the world and captivate the imagination of all who come near. But first we must remember and acknowledge this unique capacity for transformative power. Do you trust that you were created for this purpose?

Are you comfortable being and leading as the person God created you to be?

Are you willing to be who you are, vulnerable, humble, self-emptying, raw, and real?

Understanding yourself as being enough or realizing that you don't need to change who you are in order to lead effectively is one of the most essential concepts toward becoming a generational leader and creating an irresistible leadership environment that draws in the emerging generations.

I was talking with a first-time visitor to our church not too long ago. I asked her what drew her to our congregation after fifteen years of staying away from organized religion altogether. She said, "When I visited your church, it was evident that you and everyone else there were comfortable simply being yourselves, and that made it comfortable for me to be myself." I hear this frequently.

Whenever I ask members of our 20/30 groups to share what drew them to our church or to the companies they work for, they use one word in particular, *authenticity*. They tell me that the most important thing to them is that people, friends, churches, leaders, or employers are being authentic. They want to know you aren't perfect. They want to hear you laugh aloud. They want to see you cry in front of people. They want to know that you have the ability to be vulnerable. Millennials do not need fancy gimmicks, slick presentations, or lots of lights and lasers. In fact, they shy away from such things. Instead, what they are looking for is simplicity, honesty, and authenticity. It's not about the designer eyeglasses or high-end jeans, the polish or production. They are looking for raw and real, vulnerable and authentic human beings who are honest and reflective of the church's true DNA. They are looking for a kaleidoscope: a simple and straightforward tool that has the power in its simplicity to reveal the most amazing, ever-changing collage of colors.

Kaleidoscopes operate on the simple trust that something beautiful will emerge when they allow the light to shine through them. Kaleidoscopic leaders believe the same thing. When we believe that God didn't make a mistake with us and we allow the light of Christ to shine through us just as we are, then something beautiful will always emerge.

It is as simple as that.

One of my favorite scriptural stories comes from the Book of Acts. It takes place in Jerusalem in the years immediately following Jesus' death and resurrection. In Acts 8, Luke tells a story about a man named Saul, a notorious persecutor of Christians. In the eighth chapter, Saul is orchestrating the stoning of Stephen (the first Christian martyr). Scripture tells us that "Saul was ravaging the church by entering house after house; dragging off both men and women, he committed them to prison" (Acts 8:3). He breathed threats and murder against the disciples and by the ninth chapter, Saul had received papers to expand his conquest by persecuting and stamping out the Christians in neighboring Damascus.

As Saul set out for Damascus to complete his mandate, out of nowhere his life was interrupted by a bright light. The light of Christ bathed him, blinded him, and forced him to the ground. As he was on his knees in the middle of the road undoubtedly trying frantically to make sense of the light, a voice cried out, "Saul, Saul, why do you persecute me?"

Saul fearfully inquired, "Who are you, Lord?" And then the reply came, "I am Jesus, whom you are persecuting. But get up and enter the city, and you will be told what you are to do."

I love this story because a strong and powerful villain was reduced to a helpless infant, unable to see, walk, eat, or do anything without the help of another. He was rebooted—returned to the beginning when God first made him with a capacity to bear God's image for the entire world to see.

As the story continues, Saul is transformed into a powerful instrument capable of bringing the name of God before the world. After meeting with a Christ-follower named Ananias (who was instructed by God to meet with this persecutor of Christians), Saul's eyesight was restored. Saul became Paul and set out to change the world. He became a new creation full of power and might. This transformation can happen to us when we simply allow the light of Christ to shine through us.

After the ninth chapter of Acts, Paul builds churches, writes letters, suffers mightily, and boasts proudly in his weaknesses, all while proclaiming the gospel of Jesus Christ. Two thousand years later, we continue to read his letters and celebrate his history. Even today, we retrace Paul's missionary journeys, his heroic actions, and often consider him to be one of the strongest, most faithful church leaders.

I believe what made Paul great was his ability to finally be comfortable in his own skin and to simply live in such a way that allowed God's light to shine through him. He did this by rejoicing in weakness, boasting in his shortcomings. He led by telling people how he often did the things he didn't want to do and didn't do the things he did. He talked openly about his desire to die in those moments of peril so that he could simply be in heaven's embrace. Paul was able to be real. He didn't pretend. He simply allowed the light to shine through him in a raw and real fashion. God longs for us to do the very same thing.

Are you comfortable rejoicing in your weaknesses—boasting in your shortcomings, being honest about your past, being real about your present struggles and imperfections? This is the kind of courage required to change the world. Do you have all the answers or do you share with confidence your questions and doubts, trusting that regardless of who you are or how incapable you feel, God has chosen you and can use you to be an instrument of God's grace with a capacity to change the world? This is what it looks like to be a kaleidoscope: Just be you and allow the light of Christ to shine through you.

Questions for Reflection

1. Do you feel as though you are able to be "authentic" in your leadership setting? If not, where do you feel as though you are being disingenuous or inauthentic? Why?

2. Do you believe that God chose you and equipped you to reveal God's life-changing presence to the world around you?

3. Are you comfortable meeting people where they are, just as you are? If so, share a time when you were able to do this effectively. If not, what is causing your discomfort?

THE KALEIDOSCOPE EFFECT

CHAPTER 3

THE KALEIDOSCOPE LEADER

With all of the generalizations that can be made about the taste and preferences of the emerging generations when it comes to what they are looking for in a leader or in a church, there's one thing that resonates above the rest: uniqueness. If we long to meet the emerging generation where they are, then we need to have the courage to be as unique as they are. As pastors and church leaders, we must be comfortable and confident in our own skin, as people whom God created and equipped to make disciples, for a time such as this. We must remember we are created with the form and functionality of a kaleidoscope. God has chosen and equipped us to help the world around us see and experience the beautiful things of God in a way that is unique to each one of us. Therefore, in order to become leaders of institutions seeking to connect with the emerging generations, we must become kaleidoscopic in our approach to the ministry of meeting people where they are.

Have you ever used a kaleidoscope? If you have, you'll discover that its simplicity is foolproof. The beauty of a kaleidoscope is that it is designed perfectly. It never fails. Every time somebody picks one up, holds it up to the light and peers into the end, they will see a captivating array of color. And the longer one looks at this beautiful collage, the more they'll desire to continue rotating the kaleidoscope's end, because in doing so, they'll be able to witness the colors morph and move into new works of art, each more captivating than the one before. God created us in a way that resembles a kaleidoscope, and we ought to recognize the power of continuously adapting our approach toward meeting the needs of the mission fields in which we sit. Our strategy to meet and invite the emerging generations into a life-changing experience of God must not be to change or compromise who we are as leaders or individuals. We cannot simply become someone or something altogether different. That's not a strategy. Instead, we must remember who we are and begin adapting our strategy or approach. We must simply rotate and turn the dial until something beautiful emerges, and we bridge the generational gap between our church and the community.

Mechanically, this looks like being willing to constantly change and adapt our programs, invitations, and ideas in order to meet new people. As a pastor, this looks like changing our daily routines, pushing outside of our geographical comfort zones in order to find something new. The Kaleidoscopic leader is nimble, accommodating, and always trying something new without losing his or her identity, structure, or purpose. She or he is the most efficient when they are constantly tweaking and adjusting things in the hopes of accommodating the dynamic expectations of the world around them; this is when beauty emerges. Kaleidoscopic leaders take risks and often fail tremendously, but through all of the twists and turns, something beautiful will always come into focus.

When Resurrection Downtown launched, we did so with an original band of misfits. We were a motley crew with a compressed timeline. So we made decisions very quickly and with limited consideration for efficiency. Within the first month, we had decided to host our weekly worship service on Sunday evenings at 6:00 p.m. Everybody agreed on this decision, and the reason we chose that day and time was due to the fact that we "heard" this was the time most appealing for our most sought-after demographic within our mission field: the Millennial or the young professional as I referred to them.

In hindsight, this was a terrible decision. It was by all accounts the wrong time. Not only did it not match up with reality (Kansas City is a Sunday morning kind of city), but we had launched our fledgling community in a building without air-conditioning or accessible bathrooms and yet, for a season, things were working. Within our first five months, we had grown to about four hundred people worshipping at 6:00 p.m. This gave us a reason to celebrate. God was doing something extraordinary.

But then came month six and the arrival of summer. The average temperature inside of the sanctuary was somewhere in the mid-nineties. On the stage, we would top out over one hundred degrees weekly. People were passing out, nobody could pay attention, and all of our volunteers would bring three changes of clothes each weekend (one for setup, one for worship and teardown, and one to wear to dinner). It was awful . . . and Millennials were attending en masse as we thought they would. We discovered that what had initially worked was no longer working. But our failures were not reason enough to pack it up. Instead, we learned that God uses our failures in ways that will lead us forward to something more beautiful than anything we could imagine.

During that time, which I refer to as our Refining Fire, I had met a guy named Bryan. Bryan was a fourth-grade teacher and member of the emerging generation who had started attending our church after connecting with us on a couple service trips. After worshipping with us for just a few Sundays, he found himself singing the songs we sang in worship while he was working at his desk at school the following Monday. It didn't take long before one of his students overheard him singing under his breath.

"What are you singing?" the little boy asked.

"Oh, just a couple songs we sang in church yesterday."

"You go to church?"

"Yeah, I go to Resurrection Downtown."

"What's it like?"

"It's hot. See, we don't have any air-conditioning, so it's really hot in church, sometimes over one hundred degrees."

"You don't have any air-conditioning? That's not right! You gotta have air-conditioning!"

The little boy had been sitting at his desk, but eventually walked up to his teacher's desk and asked him if it would be okay if he made Bryan a fan for church.

He ended up inviting the rest of his class to join him and altogether they made over seventy hand fans. The class even laminated them and put them on sticks. The next weekend, they gifted them to me. I passed them out to the congregation only to witness this same fourth-grader, along with his teacher, Bryan, contribute a monetary offering (two dimes and three pennies) with the purpose of starting a capital campaign to purchase an air conditioner.

Six o'clock was the wrong time to launch a worship service, even though we felt initially that it was the right time to meet Millennials. We didn't waver in our service time, even as we were hemorrhaging people due to the extreme heat. We were stubborn. We thought we knew what the emerging generations were looking for, and we were failing. And yet, that was the moment when we believed that God began to use our failure in ways that would bring about a new way forward.

We formed a partnership with Bryan's school, starting with the fourth-grade class, and began inviting as many people as we could find to join us in blessing these fourth-graders in downtown Kansas City who had nothing, but were filled with so much capacity for world change. As we invited people to partner with these children, we found that our invitation was something that actually appealed to the emerging generation in ways that a worship-service time didn't.

As a result, we strategically pivoted. We adjusted our focus and strategy, and discovered something more beautiful than what we had before. We focused our invitation toward service opportunities that allowed for investment in the lives of at-risk children. This partnership paved the way for growth, new life, and hope for the future of our city by focusing on the little children in our community. The lead participants in this effort were members of the emerging generations. They served as weekly tutors, classroom readers, playground supervisors, and so much more!

This story culminated on Christmas Eve of that same year; our congregation had returned to the size we were before the summer heat. As we celebrated the light of Christ with traditional candlelight and a reading from John 1, everyone held their breath as Bryan's fourth-grader, the one who had made us hand fans in the heat of the summer just a few months earlier, ushered in the Christ candle. It was more beautiful than anything we could have imagined.

What works at first doesn't always work. When failure rears its ugly head, and it will, you cannot stop; you must adapt or turn the end of the kaleidoscope until something new emerges. Turning it might look like changing worship times or it might look like changing the invitation altogether. Whatever it is, adapting, rotating, or turning looks like remaining open to new ideas and opportunities always and everywhere.

For us, turning the kaleidoscope looked like establishing new relationships and missional strategies with several elementary schools in our neighborhood. We also began to adapt other strategies for meeting people as well. We adjusted our worship times by moving our six o'clock service on Sunday evenings to five o'clock. On top of that, we also added a morning service. At the same time, we began searching for a space solution that would allow for a better worship environment, one that was less hot with more space and working bathrooms. We were constantly seeking out ways to improve. Had we been considering our outreach in terms of kaleidoscopes, we were continually rotating the end, looking tirelessly for that next beautiful image!

The byproduct of all our tweaks and turns was a significant increase within our overall participation. We returned to the levels we were previously accustomed to before encountering the heat of the summer. Together, this experience of adapting our strategies to meet the mission field pushed our leadership team to always seek to listen first to the needs of the community before making uniform decisions based upon our perceptions of the community's need. The small turn to seek opportunities and extend invitations that people in the community would be inclined to respond to was met with a resounding yes. Kaleidoscopes will remain relevant both metaphorically and physically as long as you keep turning, rotating, and adapting them in accordance with the light.

In addition to holding a sincere disposition toward community service and a desire to invest in the lives of children, we uncovered that within the emerging generation there was also a deep longing for friendship. Each weekend in worship, and in almost every visit to the coffee shop, I would hear someone tell me how they longed *to meet people they could do life with*. The Millennials I meet aren't necessarily looking for the church in order to have place to worship, receive the sacraments, and grow in faith; they are looking to make quality friends—friends who share a similar worldview or set of values. Upon listening to this repetitive need, we as the church attempted to adapt our programming to meet them where they were in the hopes that they'd experience God through these relationships.

Initially, we collected the names and numbers of anyone who expressed a desire for meaningful relationships. We organized names of individuals who were looking to connect on a weekly basis to share life with others into groups of eight to twelve, and hosted a gathering. At that gathering, we'd walk through the importance of community life, our need to share our lives with others, and we offered training around how small groups work. We also offered curriculum and covenant agreements. Within a short period of time, we had launched several small groups involving over one hundred individuals. Each one of these groups met in homes, lofts, or community-gathering spaces around KC. We thought we had succeeded in meeting the emerging generation's desires, until they told us we hadn't.

We felt as though we were doing really well, until we began to field specific frustrations via e-mail and text from people who spoke about how these small groups weren't matching their expectations. People began to share with us how they weren't sure they liked the people they had just committed to do life with. Slowly but surely, these small groups created to meet the needs of our community were unraveling. Our "arranged marriages" were ending in divorces all over the place, and what was working no longer seemed to be doing so.

So, we adapted. We turned the kaleidoscope and changed our focus. We tried to create a low-commitment approach to community life that would allow for relationships and friendship to emerge naturally as opposed to the way we were previously seeking to manufacture them. Every two weeks, we launched what we rebranded as "community groups." A community group was a short-term study (Bible or book), with a definite start and stop that spanned anywhere between four and six weeks. Community groups were created so that anyone could drop in, sign up, drop out, or walk away at any point in time. They were an option similar to worship, in that we invited people to consider them as a way of drawing nearer to God in study and to each other in conversation.

Mechanically, we assembled a volunteer team of facilitators and leaders to host these community groups at the church building or out in the community. Every time we launched a new opportunity, we found new participants looking to connect. People would pick and choose which group to participate in based on what mattered most to them in their particular life situation. People would choose to attend a group because of its convenient location, its start time, the study material, or simply because of right "timing." By launching these groups every two weeks, we always had something new to offer anyone desiring to become a bigger part of the community.

Over the course of that next year, our community groups thrived. Moreover, the groups seemed to be comprised of every demographic within our congregation. People would not only attend these community groups to meet people they found connection with, but also inspired them or challenged them. These relationships rooted in study (Bible or book) would continue on past the initial community group, just like we had hoped.

Upon completion of their first group, participants would sign up for another study, only this time they'd do it together, or in some cases people developed friendships so quickly that they'd skip another community group and express an interest in forming a new small group. In short order, we began forming new small groups, only this time they were authentic or organic in their origin. Today we currently host approximately forty-seven small groups that meet weekly, each consisting of eight to twelve members; all of that is in addition to our ongoing community-group offerings. In retrospect, it took our strategic turn or adaptation to meet the needs within our community. By recalibrating our strategies, something beautiful emerged that we couldn't have imagined, just like a kaleidoscope.

When it came to the evolving needs of the emerging generation, one thing we learned is that for as many Millennials who desire to be surrounded by multiple generations, there is also a strong subset who longed to meet people their own age. This also presented a challenge for us, given that all of our programming was multigenerational.

In response to this challenge, we tried something new. We launched a group entitled Young and [un]Professional or "Yups" for short. Anyone who was under the age of thirtyish was invited to join this weekly community group that gathered around a book or topic-driven lesson that would eventually move toward a social outing, dinner, or coffee. From the outset, this group gained momentum quickly. We had two committed volunteers who led and coordinated the group, and within a matter of weeks we were gathering anywhere between thirty and forty young adults, all of whom were previously disconnected, but who were now engaging in study and in companionship. Adapting our approach by adding an affinity group to meet people who longed to connect with others their own age had made possible something even better than community groups, to the point that deep friendships were emerging, and in some cases more than friendships. That's when something happened that required another pivot.

About six months into this group's formation, our two leaders had fallen in love and were engaged to be married. This caused another natural, yet surprising, shift in momentum. Many of the young adults who had built relationships opted to graduate from Yups by forming or joining small groups or leaving altogether. And just like that, what had once been working stopped. And so we as Kaleidoscopic leaders adapted.

The next thing we tried was to form sports teams that were led and managed by our young adult small groups as a way of drawing people together out in the community. We began to see people who were previously disconnected entering the community on the kickball field, volleyball court, and softball diamond. We also launched a dinner club for young adults that met twice a month to try out the best restaurants in the community. We also formed a mission team and missions opportunities geared specifically for young adults so that we could meet people in soup kitchens, rebuild old homes, tend gardens, or pick up trash throughout the city.

We tried numerous new things in order to see what would connect. And whenever things didn't, we would simply turn or change directions. Our multiple failures didn't stop us from adapting or rotating just slightly in order to stumble upon or create the next beautiful thing. Most recently, we have put together a group called 20/30, and it is hosted primarily on social media, but points people to regular get-togethers ranging from coffee hours fifteen minutes before or after worship services to dialogue and discussion on theology, literature, and race. This virtual group has paved the way for a variety of connection points managed in one place in the hopes of meeting as many people possible both within the church and outside it. In a short period of time, over one hundred people have signed up to participate in a variety of these ministries. How long will it last? I don't know, but for now, it is hitting the right note. When it ceases, we'll simply adapt.

In terms of ministry with the emerging generations, permanent or static programming doesn't work. Given the age of technological advance we're in marked by perpetual software updates, upgrades, and innovation, it doesn't appear that anything lasts all that long, except that is for companies and institutions that have figured out the primary importance of change and adaptability. Think like a CEO of a Fortune 500 company that makes consumer products. You must think ahead always. In order to lead the emerging generations, we must exude an affinity for change, adaptation, and innovation. We must constantly find ways to improve our ministries. We must be willing to try new things all the time in the hopes that we'll eventually learn to speak the language that the world around us is speaking. And when at first that doesn't succeed, Kaleidoscopic leaders must continue to turn, turn, and turn, trusting that as we seek to rotate, turn, or adapt our approach, something new and beautiful will emerge, even if you cannot envision it yourself.

At times, you'll wonder if you're doing something wrong. At times, you'll feel like a failure or a square peg trying to fit into a round hole, but alas, you're not the problem. God did not make a mistake with you! You are beautifully and wonderfully made, called to change the world for such a time as this. God simply longs for you to keep trying, keep working, keep changing things up, and trusting that by the grace of God something beautiful will come forth from the dust. Get out there and meet people where they are!

Questions for Reflection

1. What ministries in your current setting are working well in terms of reaching out to the emerging generations?

2. What ministries in your setting worked well in the beginning, but have ceased to function with the same level of effectiveness?

3. What adaptations can you make in order to try something new or to tweak something old? What ministries might you need to discontinue?

4. When was the last time you tried and failed?

CHAPTER 4

SQUARE PEGS AND ROUND HOLES
(TECHNICAL CHALLENGES)

Sometimes amidst all the failure and risk-taking, Kaleidoscopic leaders will feel as though they are square pegs living in a world of round holes. To this end, God reminds us that God doesn't make mistakes in creating, calling, and equipping us for the mission at hand. That said, there are things that can leave us disconnected or unapproachable to the emerging generations. There are certain things that will render all of our efforts for evangelism and outreach moot. I consider these things to be challenges that are largely technical in nature.

There are two primary types of challenges that leaders face. There are adaptive challenges and technical challenges. Adaptive changes are generally changes in strategy and approach. Adaptive challenges involve programs, curriculum, structure, time, or topics. Adaptive challenges have everything to do with the message or our messaging.

When we shifted our branding—changed our approach to meet the emerging generations between our Young and [un] Professional group (Yups), our Dinner Group, and the 20/30 group—these were adaptive changes. In shifting our focus or rotating our approach, we continually sought to create an event, group, or invitation that people would be drawn to favorably. Kaleidoscopic leaders thrive in their willingness to tackle adaptive challenge as they live a life that runs alongside the lyrics to The Byrds' classic 1960's *Billboard* hit, "Turn! Turn! Turn!" At times, you'll fall short, but if you keep turning, you'll eventually find the life you're looking for.

On the other hand, technical challenges or operational challenges have the ability to prevent us from success, no matter how hard we try. Technical challenges don't involve the message so much as they pertain to the medium. When we think of technical challenges, we should be thinking about architecture, technology, furniture, fixtures, and equipment, and anything related to audio, visual, and lighting.

In this chapter, I hope to provide working examples of how to navigate the technical pitfalls that prevent emerging generations from paying attention or heeding direction, regardless of our willingness to face adaptive challenges head-on.

TECHNOLOGY DEPENDENT

One of the biggest misunderstandings about the emerging generation is that they actually understand the technology they use. A lot of people will refer to Millennials as being tech-savvy, implying that they understand technology or that they are brighter, more intelligent, and much more equipped to create and manage technology. I haven't found this to be true. What has been generally assumed as expertise I have discovered as dependence. The truth is that most of the emerging generation doesn't know how technology works. What they do know is that they can't do life without it. In fact, the emerging generation hasn't ever had to live without it. Technology has been a part of their life from birth. They need it, and if your church or institution doesn't involve or incorporate technology into your community, they will avoid or reject you. Like it or not, churches must meet this technical challenge by involving and incorporating as much technology as possible.

"I think this is true, but we can also pick up on if a church has a bunch of technology trying to capture us instead of creating an environment that makes us feel comfortable. Balance is key. I can see churches running with this and putting all of their money into technology and ignoring what the emerging generations really want, namely loving relationship."

Church leaders cannot expect emerging generations to drop their connectedness to modern technology simply because they enter a church!

In the sanctuary, this looks like incorporating screens into the worship space as one of the primary mediums for sharing the message. We are living in a world dominated by screens. When we want to learn, read, watch, or study, we are generally turning toward screens. Is your church screen-friendly? Many pastor friends of mine refuse to incorporate screens into their sanctuaries because they long to have a space where we can be free from them. I suppose I understand this. However, the only people who seem to want a break from screens are people who can remember a time when the only screens we watched were television and movie. This just isn't the case anymore. We have screens for our books, for our phones, for our computers, for our tablets, in our cars; and all of those are in addition to our televisions and movie theaters.

In addition to having screens, we must consider utilizing them with content that communicates in a similar fashion. It used to be that pastors would preach sermons that included three points and poem. It's funny to me in that I haven't read a book of poetry since college, however, I have watched creative poets on YouTube. I have also watched amazing, moving word art set to pencil sketches, and I have read some of the most amazing stories on the big screen. Could it be that sermons nowadays might include video elements as opposed to the traditional prose and poetry from decades ago?

"Yes!! I always wish churches used more videos even if they were silent while someone talks over them. Videos speak loudly to my generation. Videos can be seen as poetry."

In addition to having physical screens in the sanctuary, I wonder if your church is screen-friendly in the sense that you invite people to engage their screens from their seats. Most people carry their smartphones wherever they go and will check it over 265 times throughout the day.

Therefore, does your church have Wi-Fi? Do you invite people to offer feedback by way of text-message, Twitter, or Snapchat? Does your offering only involve plates and paper or can people give by means of electronic transfer, push pay, or text giving? Is your sanctuary Wi-Fi enabled? If we are seeking to meet people where they are, we can try to adapt our message or messaging, but if our mediums are out of date, unfriendly, or preventing people from living the way they are accustomed to—namely with technology—then we must meet the technical challenge by outfitting our churches, specifically our sanctuaries, to be amenable to the tech-dependent, emerging generation. If you do, what you'll discover is that even the people in your congregation who can still remember JFK's assassination will be happy because they love technology almost as much as the emerging generations do. (It's just that they needed someone to show them first!)

THE [CYBER]WORLD IS MY PARISH

Let's say your church is on board with having technology, screens, and video in the sanctuary. How is your web presence? Before most members of the emerging generation will ever make it into your church's sanctuary, they are going to visit it virtually by accessing one of their trusted screens. They'll go online to visit you on your virtual "front porch." This, of course, requires that you have a presence on the web. It is important that your church is searchable or "search engine optimized," otherwise, the emerging generations won't even know you exist.

Along with a clean, functional website, churches must have a social media platform as well (Facebook, Instagram, and so forth). Do you have a profile? Does it reflect your identity, values, and reality? Are there pictures? videos? Can I see myself in your congregation? Does your community engage the world around you, and not just in your neighborhood you find yourself, but in and throughout the virtual community as well? This is necessary. Before the emerging generations visit, they want to see that you are as tech-dependent as they are, and then it is imperative that whatever they might see online will look to be just as unique as they are. The emerging generations will not see a church without any sort of web presence. If you cannot check in at your church, offer a Yelp review or Google it; I argue that few Millennials will find you.

APPROACHABLE AND EASILY ACCESSIBLE

Given that Resurrection Downtown's first building was a former bar/concert venue, approaching our church felt as familiar as entering any restaurant or bar in the neighborhood. Our church looked like our neighborhood. Our entry looked like everybody else's entry and, therefore, there is no lack of familiarity when it comes to going to church at Resurrection Downtown. In fact, one of the things that people have said time and time again after their first visit was how easy it was to find and how comfortable it feels upon entering. Because Millennials are considered the first unchurched generation, the first impression of entering into a very traditional, vaulted building can feel unapproachable.

Additionally, Millennials' decisions to become involved in churches can also hinge on our building's accessibility. This means that in order to actually enter the church, everything must be easily identifiable, well lit, clearly marked, and accommodate persons with special needs.

It is important to pay attention to how our spaces communicate. The overwhelming majority of the emerging generation enters a church for the very first time seeking community. Are your first-impression spaces open to community engagement and connection? Is there open space to gather, to connect, to drink coffee? So many older churches had defined rooms for connection or halls reserved for coffee.

What if you could transform the entire church building—
hallways, classroom, even the sanctuary—into one big space
for building community? Where can you make soft spaces
with tables and chairs, stations throughout the church for
coffee and tea, music playing throughout so that everywhere
you turn you might find someone to sit with, chat with, drink
with? In the event that is not possible, then what would it do
to have clear signs and volunteers leading the way to such
spaces? Without space for community and connection, it
doesn't matter how much you try; your message will have a
difficult time getting through.

In the same way, any type of separation between the sacred
and the ordinary will serve as an unwelcome barrier as well.
When interviewing a group of Millennials about what they
look for upon visiting a church for the very first time, the
unanimous response was coffee.

"Amen!"

They wanted to know if they would be able to take coffee into
the sanctuary. This is important for the emerging generation
because this communicates a word of welcome, and this goes
especially for good coffee. The emerging generation has only
ever known a reality where there is a Starbucks on every
corner. They grew up knowing that America runs on Dunkin'.
Coffee is staple of everyday life. The emerging generations
hashtag *pumpkin spice lattes* in the fall. They look forward to
the green and red cups at Christmastime, and they long to
have their iced frappuccinos in the summer and iced coffees in
the springtime. This is a generation steeped in coffee culture.
They drink coffee at work, at home—everywhere they go—so
they will expect to be able to do so at church as well. When
they have coffee, they have their comfort. A pastor could be
wearing a robe, the choir could be in the loft, you could be

singing out of a hymnal, but if there were coffee, all would be right in the world. If there isn't coffee, . . .

REDUCE, REUSE, RECYCLE

The last major technical challenge that Kaleidoscopic leaders must face upon seeking to lead the emerging generations into a future filled with hope has everything to do with the environment. How your physical structures and footprint deal with matters of environmental stewardship is imperative to the younger generations. Millennials are focused squarely on matters of climate control, global warming, and civic responsibility. They want to do their part. The emerging generations pay attention to how green their church is. You must be cognizant of their priority when it comes to doing your part in caring for creation. Does your church communicate this effectively? physically? Do you have recycle bins? Do you use Styrofoam cups? Do you have a million inserts in your weekly bulletin? Do you have a weekly bulletin?

"Millennials don't care about bulletins! We can go online to get whatever we need."

Not paying attention to how your building and resources impact God's creation feels hypocritical to a generation focused on stewarding all that has been given to us. The psalmist writes, "The earth is the Lord's and everything in it." If written today, the Millennial might add, "And God has given it to us to enjoy to its fullest." Part of enjoying creation is caring for it, and this is something that should resonate with every single church building. What can you do to make your building "green"? Perhaps it's as simple as adding bike racks (both inside and outside of your building) as a means of promoting and welcoming alternate modes of transportation. Many churches have started community gardens and/or compost areas to promote better awareness of what goes into our bodies and what it takes to produce what we eat. Other ideas include putting solar panels on your roof, installing low-flow toilets, replacing traditional light bulbs with LEDs, or even just adding motion sensors on your light switches. These modifications to your physical structure might make all the difference.

Kaleidoscopic leaders turn, turn, and turn, trusting that something beautiful will emerge when it comes to meeting people where they are. A great leader will adapt strategy and approach in order to invite people into an encounter with the living God, and throughout this process failure will inevitably abound as we miss the mark. However, failure doesn't mean that you need to give up and throw away the whole kaleidoscope. Even though leaders may feel like a square peg in a round hole from time to time, you are not. The God of the universe wonderfully and creatively made you for a time and a task such as this. However, if you are not paying attention to the technical challenges facing you and your ministry—things like physical structure, the use of technology, architecture, and accents—then you'll find that any effort in meeting people where they are will fall short, as there are some technical barriers that will separate us from the mission of inviting the emerging generations into an encounter with the living God.

Questions for Reflection

1. What are the greatest technical challenges facing your ministry or leadership environment?

2. How have you/can you incorporate technology into your community?

3. Do you have an easily accessible/approachable church community for people who aren't already connected to the rhythms of faith?

4. Is your ministry conscious of the environmental factors?

CHAPTER 5

CULTIVATING AND SUSTAINING IRRESISTIBLE LEADERSHIP ENVIRONMENTS (WHAT'S REQUIRED)

In the last chapter, I mentioned the technical barriers to meeting and ministering to the needs of the emerging generations. We must pay attention to our structure, how we use our physical spaces, the way we impact the environment, our connection to available technology, and our online presence in general. Paying attention to these technical challenges will positively impact our connection with the emerging generations and minimize our propensity to feel as though we are square pegs living in a world of round holes. However, in addition to overcoming these operational or technical challenges, there are five additional things we must consider doing consistently in order to cultivate and sustain irresistible leadership environments for the emerging generations.

Irresistible leadership environments are spaces with an atmosphere that facilitates effective emotional, relational, spiritual, and theological connections with God and with one another. Irresistible leadership environments tend to possess five primary facets. They are: **hospitality, anonymity, authenticity, mystery,** and **creativity**. In this chapter, we will explore these five primary facets and at the same time, offer up some how-to components of what it takes to create compelling environments for the emerging generations.

HOSPITALITY

I was spending time over coffee with a 29-year-old father of two who had only recently started attending our church, and during our conversation he shared his criteria for finding a space to worship. He said, "When I walk into a church, I want to see a group of people who are unafraid to welcome and greet everyone the same way, regardless of who they are or where they've come from, regardless of age, gender, sexual orientation, or anything else for that matter."

Implied in his comment was that this same church (in addition to demonstrating radical hospitality) would also reflect that through diversity within the makeup of the worshipping congregation. In other words, this young man was expressing a desire to be a part of a congregation that welcomed people, engaged people, loved people (all people), equally regardless of where they come from or what they've been through. And this must be reflected within the physical makeup of the congregation.

"YES!! I always have such a hard time with the fact that churches are segregated. How does that reflect God at all? I 100% will go to a church if it is diverse. If it isn't, I will talk about it and how this must change."

Emerging generations seek out environments where they are noticed, welcomed, and made to feel at home. This looks like having multiple encounters where people can say, "Hello!" offer their "Good Mornings!" and remind others multiple times throughout the hour, "We're so glad you're here." Being made to feel welcome and included is imperative because when you are made to feel at home, you are more likely to be open and available to have an experience of God. A part of this happens through greetings, handshakes, and a general culture of camaraderie, but this also happens when worship leaders remember to model this in their leadership of the worship service itself.

Opening up the service of worship with a simple compliment reinforcing your appreciation of their presence is just one simple way to extend hospitality into the worship service itself. I begin every single worship service at Resurrection Downtown the same way. I say, "Thank you for joining us in worship today and for choosing this to be where you experience God today. I don't know where you have come from or what you've gone through in order to be here today, but I am so glad that you are here. And because you're here, my hope is that you would meet God here today!"

My goal in worship is to make people feel welcome; I want to help them to feel at home. Once I do, I remind them of our hope: that they might meet God here in this place with all of these people, regardless of who they are or what they've been through. I say this up front. I also make the same announcement in the middle of our service immediately before prayer because I recognize that most first-time visitors and most of the members of the emerging generation don't always show up on time. They often show up fifteen minutes late. One of the defining characteristics of the emerging generation is realizing that being on time means anytime within the first fifteen minutes of the slated start time. So, being hospitable requires words of greeting and welcome multiple times from the front of stage, in addition to the multiple times before and after the worship services. (Also, this is a given—one mustn't get offended whenever someone shows up late. Instead of taking offense, one should give thanks according to the mantra, "Better late than never.")

I've discovered that when I live with a hope for a divine encounter and a desire to welcome people home as they walk through the doors of Resurrection Downtown regardless of their age, appearance, past experience, or time of service, people will gather together, increasing numbers in beautifully diverse ways. This only happens if the worshipping congregation is made to believe that everybody (church leaders, church members, and first-time visitors) is actually there for the same reason, to meet God. This is hospitality.

But being hospitable is only one of five facets that work together to make up an irresistible leadership environment. Hospitality simply gets people in the door and helps them to feel comfortable and available in worship.

ANONYMITY

In the same way that everyone must be welcomed, recognized, and made to feel at home, churches and their leaders must also cultivate a feeling of anonymity within the environment.

My younger sister, Jill, works for Google. She's approaching her thirties and because her brother is a pastor, she has felt inclined to visit churches with the hopes of finding a place where she can meet the living God. She has shared with me multiple stories of her visits to area churches. She will often describe a church's ability to make her feel welcome, only to cross a line and later drive her away. Jill says in an attempt to be friendly and get to know her, churches will inevitably seek to secure some sort of commitment from her too early. She's been asked to be a part of a Young Adults Group, a church IT team, a NextGen team, SPRC, and several other committees too numerous to mention; and all of this after having visited these churches only one time. I suspect my sister's experience of visiting churches is fairly consistent with much of the emerging generations.

There is an urgency fueling churches these days. Churches are so eager to welcome young people that in their welcome, they too quickly move into pleas for deep commitment. That is sensory overload. What's counterintuitive about this kind of approach is that in their haste to be welcoming, churches and their leaders are actually compromising their ability to be hospitable. In the hopes of securing participation and involvement from younger people, they end up singling out an entire segment of the population. Young adults leave feeling as though the church doesn't actually want them there in the hopes that they could meet God; they want them there simply to help them grow the church. This is self-serving, alienating, and isolating, rather than hospitable. It forces young people into a place where they feel as though they are standing out in a crowd, even more than they already are. This becomes especially harmful because oftentimes, these same churches don't apply the same type of urgency or expectation to every first-time visitor, just the young adults. You generally don't see this same kind of welcome extending to the men and women off the street, to the widow, or to the middle-aged mom or dad. Their general critique is often the opposite of the young adult, namely that churches don't expect enough from me.

After several failed attempts at finding the "right" church, my sister shared with me that she longs to become a part of a church that is friendly and hospitable to all people, regardless of where they come from or what they've been through. But she wants her church to also foster a sense of anonymity. Meaning, she wants to be welcomed and made to feel at home and then she wants to be able to hide, to be anonymous, or free to go at her own pace or sink into the rhythm and practices of the church. She longs for anonymity.

A key to facilitating anonymity is preserving a sense of personal privacy within the worshipping congregation. In order to accomplish this, there are several things leaders can do beyond restraining your desire to secure deep commitment from Millennials after their first encounter. Leaders can create anonymity or personal privacy by tweaking the worship service in ways that allow everyone to be on the same page, regardless of their past experiences. This is imperative to understand because there are a lot of customs and rituals that happen in worship that don't happen anywhere else in the world.

If you stop to think about it, the church is the only place where people are invited to sing aloud to songs they do not know in front of total strangers without the aid of some mood-altering substance. This is something most church leaders take for granted. This is not normal. It used to be normal. My grandpa used to tell me stories from his days in the military where the guys in his barracks used to sing together to pass the time. He told me how his fraternity used to write songs and serenade the neighboring sororities frequently and how jingles were written to sell products, elect candidates, and introduce the best shows on television. This doesn't happen anymore. Yet we invite people to sing in public every weekend in front of strangers without any explanation or context. In this way, the church is a place that challenges our preconceived notions of what is normal from a societal perspective given our expectations of what people do in the midst of worship.

Singing hymns or unfamiliar songs is just one of the unusual demands we ask of our worshipping congregation and any first-time visitor. Additionally, we have people regularly stand up, sit down, and sometimes kneel over the course of an hour. In that same time, we'll invite people to introduce themselves to perfect strangers. We'll instruct them to "pass the peace"; we have people put their money in a plate that passes by; and we have them take bread, dip it into a cup of grape juice, and eat it. In worship, we have people do all of these things that don't happen anywhere else in their daily lives and hope they feel comfortable doing so. In order for this to happen, we need to create a sense of anonymity. People must be made to feel comfortable in worship by thinking that nobody is watching, and they must be given proper instruction to the extent that they know the importance of why we do the things we do and how to do them so that they won't draw any unwarranted attention by participating.

One of the easiest ways congregations can seek to create this sense of anonymity is by taking measures to dim the sanctuary lights so that visibility within the congregation is reduced. In a low-lit sanctuary, worship participants can experience an environment where one might feel free to cry, laugh, sing, or even fall asleep without the fear of everyone noticing, including the pastor. Movie theaters are a great example of this. The lights go down in the theater, and immediately you feel free to experience a different narrative for a two- to three-hour period of time. Churches can learn from this. However, in addition to dimming the sanctuary lights, increasing the light levels on the chancel or stage will do the same thing. It will preserve anonymity by drawing all attention forward, and using a centrally located screen or pulpit will enhance our focus toward the front and reduce the distraction of wandering eyes.

Boosting volume within the sanctuary has the same effect. If there are ways you can help people to sing, it's by drowning their fear of being heard with a loud house.

Another way to create a space where one can feel anonymous is through the use of context or over-explaining all movement and activity within the worship service. One of the easiest ways to be noticed as an outsider in a worship service occurs every time someone is unsure of what he or she is supposed to do or how they should act. Context is how we explain and offer instruction as to the how and why of what we do. Worship leaders should introduce the songs we sing with a backstory and inspired intentionality as to why they chose this song for worship. Similarly, pastors should take responsibility for explaining the importance of prayer before inviting congregations to pray and display the words to any congregational prayers or recited creed.

Finally, we should unpack the offering as opposed to passing the plates and expecting people to instinctively know what to do. These are simple ways to help people blend in, feel comfortable, and allow them to understand the why and how of worship so that they can participate fully without drawing undue attention upon themselves.

AUTHENTICITY

We've discussed the emerging generation's deep need for authenticity or vulnerability in leaders. The desire is reflected in our worship space as well. Therefore, as leaders inviting people to experience the grace of Jesus Christ, we should approach worship not as a leader set apart from the congregation but instead as the lead worshipper.

Every time we worship as pastors or leaders, we ought to lead by example. We must come as we are, acknowledging that God is God and we are not, saying, like Isaiah, "Woe is me, I am a man of unclean lips." This is authenticity.

Kaleidoscopic leaders must be comfortable in their own skin. They must demonstrate authenticity, vulnerability, or transparency with ease. They must have an amazing propensity for meeting the emerging generation, speaking a language they can understand. Authenticity is what they are looking for more than anything else. We can model this in worship by seeking to communicate with truthful and sincere candor. We must be comfortable in our own skin. We must be as unique and as flawed as they are. Pastors and leaders who are trying to play it cool by simply saying the right things, listening to the right music, or wearing the right clothes are easily identified as playing cool as opposed to being cool.

> "I wish leaders stopped acting like they are different or better than everyone else. We are all children of God, and that should never be forgotten. How powerful it is to know that a leader is in the same boat as everyone else."

At Resurrection Downtown, we train our worship leaders to think of themselves as being the leaders of awkward encounters. We inevitably make mistakes; we will say the wrong things at the wrong times, and we acknowledge and embrace it. We are not perfect. Ask anyone in Kansas City, and they'll share with you that Resurrection Downtown is a church full of misfits.

This is at least a part of the reason why they come to church. They want to get to a place where they can become naked and unafraid, where they can simply be the best versions of the people God created them to be. For Jesus, this looked like a life defined by the practice of self-emptying. Paul referred to Jesus' power as being found in his willingness to take the form of a slave, even though he had the power of God. Authenticity requires an ongoing admission of shortcomings and an unwavering openness to learning and growing from everyone and every situation you encounter. Humble leaders or authentic leaders are not dominating, polished, or perfected personalities. They are catalysts for authentic environments.

The emerging generation wants environments where they are comfortable sharing who they are—their fears, their doubts, their insecurities, their celebrations with the Living God who has the power to meet them, inspire them, and transform them into the best versions of the people God created them to be. This can happen when leaders have the courage to not only facilitate the space for it, but embody it themselves.

If we long to invite people to come as they are, then we must be willing to do the same. We must be willing to come to worship just as we are. This is authenticity. This is what draws emerging generations closer to God because it allows them to feel safe being open in the same way. So, make mistakes, don't script transitions, and live into every invitation you extend to the congregation. If you invite people to pray silently, then you better do the same thing. If you challenge people in sermons with action steps, then you better take them too. If you invite people to experience God's presence in communion, then you must also treat that as a worship experience in your own life, not just as something to provide or make possible as a leader. And then in the moments you fail, share about your experience in falling short.

MYSTERY

At the same time we acknowledge the importance of authenticity in creating an irresistible leadership environment for emerging generations, we must also acknowledge our need for something much greater than we are. We must create space in our churches for the God of the universe, the Holy Mystery in which we cannot fully comprehend, understand, or even imagine. Within the church, we describe sacraments as the primary pathways for us to experience the power of God's promises. We can experience the life-saving power of God through baptism and Holy Communion.

Sacrament comes from the Latin word *sacramentum*, which is a term most commonly understood to mean "promise." A sacrament is a promise of God. Through the sacraments of baptism and Holy Communion, we experience God's promises. Through the sacraments, God promises us and actually gives us life that never ever ends. But how this actually happens is a total mystery. I've always found the element of mystery particularly interesting. Did you know that a sacrament translated in Ancient Greek is *mysterion*? In Greek, this term means exactly what it looks like. The sacraments and how they convey God's power and grace are a holy mystery.

"I wish the church talked about this mystery more often. I think it speaks to people of all generations and is something that Millennials are genuinely searching for."

There are a variety of explanations that attempt to unpack exactly how this works, but largely when it comes to God's promises and the inner-workings of God's grace, it is a divine mystery.

Incorporating the divine mystery into worship is imperative. Doing so points us to the one thing everybody needs and the only thing that has the power to transcend every generation throughout all of creation, namely the grace of God. How are you inviting mystery, the power and promises of God, into your worship services?

Are the sacraments present and offered with regularity?

Jesus says, "Go therefore, and make disciples of all nations, baptizing them in my name." At the Last Supper, on the night in which he gave himself over to the Roman authorities for us, Jesus instructed his disciples to "Take. Eat. Drink. And every time you do, I want you to remember me." Sacraments are the promises of God that Jesus commands us to participate in as often as possible, so that we might remember Jesus, experience the life that we're looking for, and invite others to experience the same thing.

Baptism and Communion are the grand channels through which the earliest of Christians traveled down in order to connect with God's life-saving power. Baptism and Communion should be the same for us as well. At Resurrection Downtown, we participate in the sacrament of Holy Communion every weekend in every worship service in order that we have an opportunity to invite people into an experience of the mystery of God's amazing grace that transcends our humanity, authenticity, and best effort. Often, before we invite people to experience Holy Communion, we remind people that God longs to meet us, fill us, use us, and in the moments we don't get it right, God will oftentimes move in spite of us in order to change the world. This usually starts at the Lord's Table, where Christ invites us all to come just as we are, as imperfect as we feel, to experience the two things we all need: God's grace and mercy.

Do your worshipping environments point people to participate in something greater than you? Do you consistently invite the holy mystery of God's promise of eternal life into your church? Do you invite people to travel down the grand channels of faith that extend beyond the here and now? This is something that the emerging generation, actually, every generation longs for—a foretaste of thy kingdom come here on earth just as it is in heaven. If you don't do this, what's holding you back?

CREATIVITY

After the Last Supper in the Gospel of John, Jesus invites the disciples to go and do the same things that he has first done for them. He reminds his disciples, saying, "Those who believe in me will do the things that I do, even greater things. They will know you are my disciples because of your love for one another." Jesus' love makes possible new life. The love of Christ paves the way for new life; in this way we are called to do the same thing in our lives and in our worship. We are called to breathe new life by living and loving the same way that Christ first does for us. I define this as creativity.

Resurrection Downtown began as a collection of nine individuals, but we quickly grew into a community numbering in the thousands of people. Our vision was to transform the heart of the city authentically, passionately, and perhaps most importantly, creatively. We wanted to be known for doing the same things that Christ did; we wanted to become co-creators. As this took shape and we began to grow, something really amazing started happening. More and more artists and musicians began gravitating toward our emerging community. As a result, we tried to find ways to invite and incorporate these increasing levels of creativity.

One of the ideas we had was to take the exterior wall of our church building and transform it into a blank canvas for the community. We put out a "request for proposal," inviting the most creative people in KC (and within our congregation) to display what Resurrection Downtown looked like to them. We also opened up our sanctuary walls in the hopes that they might become gallery walls or what we imagined as modern-day stained glass, inspired by local artists. The byproduct of all of this was that our worship services have become a place where every month, people from the community introduce some of the most amazing fabric, oil, print, and photography. Over the past several years, we have found ourselves in a worship space that is clearly open to the everyday creativity, dreams, and wonder about how God is calling us to become the best versions of the people we were created to be.

It has been amazing to see this unfold naturally. Creativity speaks in ways that the emerging generation seems to understand more than most. In addition to artists, several musicians have joined us as well. Our musicians have come largely because our community offered them an opportunity to employ the gifts they had been given as well. To the extent that we might experience the grace of God together through new creative expressions, it was only natural that musicians began writing and composing music to be incorporated into our worship experience as well. The result has been beautiful worship that not only fulfills our volunteer musicians, but it stirs the heart of everyone gathered with authentic lament, praise, and singing. What's better is that these musicians have all become friends, and they believe that the best way to glorify God is by sharing everything they've been given. This is what rests at the heart of Glory Revival. Glory Revival is, for our artists, a vision of a way forward.

Artists and musicians and the emerging generation can see things that others cannot. In that way, artists have the ability to lead the way forward. In the same way that farmers plow the land in order to cultivate a ripe harvest, artists plow the landscape of our cities in order that a vibrant and creative community might take root.

Glory Revival is a collective of artists and thinkers rooted in downtown Kansas City who are a part of the fastest-growing urban church within mainline Protestantism. These members of the emerging generation see it as their calling to share what they've experienced in a way that collaborates and invites others to do the same. What if you could do the same?

Questions for Reflection

1. How does your leadership environment or ministry setting embody the five primary facets for creating irresistibility?

2. What are your community's top strengths? Where are your areas for greatest improvement?

3. Based on your current practices, what would you characterize as the five primary facets of your leadership environments?

4. What needs to change?

to be best in
point of view
Empathy
understand
feelings, th
of another

CHAPTER 6

MEASURING YOUR LEADERSHIP EFFECTIVENESS

Today's church leader, just like any leader, must constantly find ways to improve. A foundational strategy toward improving invites ongoing evaluation and feedback. Great leaders become who they are not by having the right answers, but by having the courage to ask the right questions of others. Are you inviting feedback? Are you asking the right questions of others? Are you asking your congregations' opinions, inviting their thoughts, or opening yourself up to new insights? Are you doing this within the broader community? What about with your family? Great leaders acknowledge that they don't have the market cornered when it pertains to having all the answers. Instead, they are constantly seeking feedback and longing to grow by asking questions of others.

One of the things that the emerging generation understands is that in a Google society, we no longer have all the answers. If you don't know something, we ask Google's opinion. If you don't know something, we ask Siri for help. This is a recent phenomenon that has made possible a new kind of leader, a humble leader who acknowledges she or he cannot possibly have all the answers and therefore must rely upon the expertise of others. This style of leadership makes possible a more excellent way forward that not only has the capacity to accomplish extraordinary results, but builds community and trust along the way.

This is a recent phenomenon. It used to be that leaders were leaders because they were experts. The Wharton School (one of the top business schools in the world) opened in 1881. It used to be that with a master of business and administration (MBA), graduates could jump past the factory floor right into management. Those at the top of the organization had more knowledge than those underneath them. The same can't be said now, at least with any degree of certainty. Technology has put knowledge in the hands of anyone with access to a computer (approximately 76 percent of the US population). Most employees in the workforce know more than their leaders do about their job. Nowadays, leaders are finding themselves leading people who do things they cannot understand, meaning they can't possibly have all the answers, which means that leaders today have to be comfortable using questions to increase others' alignment, engagement, and accountability.

This is one of the most difficult challenges leaders are facing with the emerging generation, namely accepting that you may not know what is right, or best, for most situations. However, this is a way of life for the emerging generation. So, one of the best ways to increase and improve your capacity for leadership also becomes one of the best ways to meet and invite the emerging generation into your community.

For the emerging generation, this propensity for deeper understanding and ongoing development through continual feedback is essential, a foundational rhythm of a life worth living. Things are changing so fast; there are so many different players, so many different scales, and so many different competing environments. The answers you knew to be true yesterday or today might not be relevant tomorrow. Given today's pace of technological change, the 24-hour news cycle, and the corresponding trending topics, it is literally impossible to have all the answers, and so we must be comfortable with questions.

In order to become a Kaleidoscopic leader for generations to come, we must be comfortable asking questions of others and inviting feedback. We must become like Thomas, the disciple. Thomas was a leader who was comfortable asking questions. Being a pastor in Missouri, I usually refer to Thomas as Missouri's own "Show Me" disciple. Most churchgoers know Thomas as someone who had a lot of useless questions, not as a disciple or faithful follower. We generally consider Thomas to be less than, as opposed to someone we should look up to. And yet throughout the Gospels, it was Thomas's questions that led to a renewed understanding of the life of faith, not simply for Thomas, but for everyone around him. A Kaleidoscopic leader should look a lot like Thomas: comfortable in his or her own doubt and lack of expertise, but at the same time courageous enough to ask questions of those around him or her.

In John 14, Jesus told his disciples about how he was leaving them and where he was planning on going. However, in sharing this news, Jesus didn't give the disciples his forwarding address or any other clues as to where he'd be going. What made this worse for the disciples was that Jesus thought they knew. He concluded his conversation with the disciples by saying casually, "And don't worry, you know the way to the place where I'm going." But they didn't.

Every other disciple stood there nodding his head, pretending to know what Jesus was talking about, but Thomas had no idea. In his confused state, he refused to go along with the crowd and separated himself from the others by saying, "No! Jesus, we don't know the way to the place where you're going. You're going to have to show us!" Thomas's question pushed Jesus for answers, deeper understanding, and a clear pathway forward to help them get to where he was going. In response, Jesus shared with them a new commandment of love, saying, "Love one another the way I have loved you . . . by this people will know you, and by doing this you'll be able to meet me where I'm going." Thomas's questions uncovered the pathway of love that would lead him to the life he was looking for. This is the power leaders can discover when they have the courage to ask questions.

Thomas didn't stop at one question either. Thomas demonstrated the same kind of questioning courage in John 20, when the disciples claimed Jesus had returned from the grave. Without Thomas's vulnerability to ask the question nobody else was willing to ask, by demanding proof, "Unless I see his hands and touch his side, I will not believe," none of the other disciples would have been able to see the fullness of God's love. Again, it was by asking the question that Thomas found life and helped others to experience the same thing.

Questions pave the way toward life. Our comfort in not knowing the right answers will lead us to renewed understanding and life, and help those around us to experience the same. Questions are essential to leading the church for generations to come.

Jim Lowry, biblical scholar, says, "Raw hope begins when you have the courage to question, the courage to deal with your honest doubts." Thomas is not thrown out of the community because of them, but he is accepted by our Lord, questions and all.[3]

---

3. Joseph S. Harvard, Sermon: "Practicing Resurrection Faith," First Presbyterian Church (Durham, NC. April 7, 2013).

Thomas wasn't afraid of looking foolish; his desire to grow pushed him past conventional wisdom in a way that he would never have been able to had he not asked honest questions. This is how we ought to live and lead as well, but not simply because of Thomas's witness. This was Jesus' way as well.

If you look to the Gospels, you'll discover that Jesus asked 307 questions throughout his ministry. That's a lot of questions. In a world that seeks certainty, it would seem that Jesus' mission and ministry offered a different way forward. What does it mean that Jesus, the Son of God, asked so many questions?

Jesus also fielded a lot of questions. Throughout the Gospels, he was asked 183 questions. However, more fascinating than that is that out of all the questions he received, Jesus only answered three of them. Jesus wasn't an answer man; he led instead by asking questions of those around him.

What does it mean to our walk of faith or our role as church leader that Jesus asked so many questions?

Our curiosity and willingness to ask the right questions are pivotal toward becoming the best versions of the people God created us to be. If you look to TV or social media, you'll find countless examples of the opposite. You'll find game shows and quizzes that reward contestants who know the answers to preset trivial questions. You can win a million dollars or earn a top-level scholarship to the college of your choice by having encyclopedic knowledge. Similarly, you can master *The Book of Discipline of the United Methodist Church* and *Robert's Rules of Order* and become authoritative as a leader, but I can assure you that simply knowing the answers won't make you a leader others will follow. Having all the knowledge in the world won't offer you the life that really is life. That prize, the best prize, goes to the ones who are willing to ask more questions and to the people who commit to learning more and faster than those who already feel as though they have all the prescribed answers.

Jesus asked questions, and so should we.

One great example of a business leader who understands the power of questions is Elon Musk. As the founder of Tesla Motors and creator of one of the most highly rated electric vehicles (one accolade amongst a long list of technological achievements), Musk understands the power and importance of asking questions. In an interview about his successful resume of inventions, Musk was asked about where his forward-thinking, innovative ideas come from. He replied, "Just trying really hard—the first order of business is to try. You must try until your brain hurts."[4]

You see, ever since college Musk had this vision of commercializing electric vehicles for the mass market, but he was reluctant to do so at first because (at the time) building electric cars was considered to be in his own words, "one of the stupidest things you could do."[5] At the time, traditional car companies were operating under two publicly agreed-upon pretenses. The first: One cannot create a compelling electric car. The second: Even if you did, no one would buy it.

Musk's journey began when he had the courage to question these underlying assumptions, and the result was astonishing. Tesla's Model S was rated the number one car ever tested by Consumer Reports, and it hasn't ended there. Since the Model S, Tesla has produced an SUV as well as a consumer car, the Model 3, which only costs $35,000. This happened because Musk was willing to ask the questions, to challenge the prevailing assumptions.

4. Paul J.H. Schoemaker and Steven Krupp, "The Power of Asking Pivotal Questions," *MIT Sloan Management Review,* Winter 2015, http://sloanreview.mit.edu/article/the power-of-asking-pivotal-questions/
5. Ibid.

Strategic leaders are focused on the future. They are masters of discerning the right questions to ask, and exploring ideas and options that are outside of the mainstream. They are weary of the status quo and prefer honest, transparent questions that are focused solely on how to make things better. This is an underlying principle guiding most start-up companies, this was Jesus' preferred way toward transformation, and this ought to be the church's as well. As we seek to become Kaleidoscopic leaders for generations to come, we must strive to meet and invite the emerging generation into the conversation with questions.

As you imagine life as a leader who leads with questions, I would like to share three ways that I have sought to incorporate questions into my ministry at Resurrection Downtown. They're pretty simple. First, we ask questions of God in prayer for direction, insight, and wisdom. Secondly, we ask questions of our staff, including volunteer leadership teams, for feedback and how to implement ministry. Finally, we ask questions of those we want to serve to know their needs and how we're doing. Identifying the right questions and the right people is essential in order to secure the legitimacy of your current leadership capacity, as well as your potential leadership capacity within your community.

As someone who strives to press on toward the goal of building Christian community where nonreligious and nominally religious people are becoming deeply committed, I have tried to focus regularly on inviting feedback and critique. I generally begin by asking God questions through prayer.

QUESTION GOD

One of the best ways to invite transformation and change into your leadership ability and potential is to ask God continually for guidance and direction through prayer. Prayer is holy conversation with the purpose of developing a relationship with God the Father, Son, and Holy Spirit.

Teresa of Avila viewed mental prayer as nothing more than an intimate sharing between friends, which requires that we take time frequently to be alone with God who we know loves us. The important thing in prayer is not to think too much, but to love much, and do that which best stirs you to love, always remembering that love is not a great delight, but rather a great desire to please God in everything. In prayer, we ask, "God, what would be pleasing unto you?" And in reply, God assures us, saying, "This is."

When we are able to think about prayer as a way of communicating with God in the hopes of developing an ever-deepening relationship, we will become more effective in our leadership. Prayer is not the spiritual equivalent to rubbing a genie's lamp. It is building a love-filled relationship with God. If you've ever initiated a friendship, you'll know that sometimes in the beginning, it can feel a little awkward. Forming a relationship begins as we attempt to figure each other out. However, over time it becomes natural and generally grows until you feel like you could talk for hours. This is how prayer should lead us as well. So that in those moments when life is unraveling before our eyes, we would know exactly how to pray.

Through prayer, we can prepare ourselves for the times when we walk through really difficult situations—moments when we feel like there is no one to talk to, no one who understands us, or when we are just desperate. In those moments, our instinct is to simply cry out to God. This only happens if we engage God first with all we have and all we are. It doesn't matter if it feels awkward or natural; we must develop the discipline to ask questions of God in a daily fashion if we're going to grow in relationship and stature as a leader.

To make it simple and easily replicable, I seek God's daily guidance by asking three questions of God in prayer:

1. Lord, what must I start doing today in order to be a better leader today than I was yesterday?

2. Lord, what must I stop doing in order to make room for new life, new opportunities, and new adventures within my ministry today?

3. Lord, what should I continue doing as a way of living into our mission of meeting people where they are with the life-changing power of God?

By asking these questions regularly, I have begun to shape my posture toward activities that are pleasing to God. These activities have in turn helped me to lead more effectively and faithfully in accordance with God's will for my life.

In addition to prayer, I have tried to adapt these three questions so that they also become the filter through which I read Scripture. John Wesley was known for saying, "All who desire the love of God are to wait for it in searching the Scriptures." If we desire to increase in our capacity to lead and love like God, then we ought to spend time searching for it in the Scriptures. Scripture is a gift and a tool for us to read and remember how deep God's love for us actually is.

When I read Scripture, I read it to remember that God pursues us relentlessly, regardless of what we have done or left undone. I read it to remember that God is always pushing and inspiring us with new ways to grow into the best version of the leader that God created us to be, image-bearers or ambassadors for Christ. I regularly ask myself: How are you bearing God's image to the world around you?

In order to answer the questions of purpose and mission, we must wrestle with Scripture by asking questions as a filter by which we read. When we read an account of Christ's crucifixion, we should wonder things like, "What does it mean that Jesus offered forgiveness to those hanging beside him on the cross?" Then we should ask, "How should I respond to this story? What should I do in light of this? What should I stop doing?"

When we read through the Gospels and Jesus' countless journeys, interruptions, and surprise suppers, it is imperative for church leaders to wonder about the present-day implications. What does it mean that Jesus rarely spent time inside the walls of the temple? What does it mean to our church's mission that Jesus found every opportunity to dine with tax collectors and sinners? Kaleidoscopic leaders should constantly ask God, "What should I stop doing in light of your story?" We should also ask, "God, what do I need to start doing in light of who you are and what you do?"

As people seeking to become generational leaders, are you looking simply for encyclopedic knowledge, the right answers, or are you seeking to ask the right questions? Do you want to continue growing and developing in ways that draw you into a better version of the leader you are today?

I urge you to spend time in prayer, asking God for guidance. Ask those same questions as you read Scripture, and continually invite God's feedback and suggestions as to how you ought to grow closer to God in all that you say and do, to the end that you might become a clearer reflection of God's image as one of God's disciples or ambassadors.

QUESTION THE STAFF

In addition to inviting God's feedback and critique through prayer and Scripture, I also strive to ask questions and seek the ongoing counsel of my staff team. This has been one of the most important aspects of growing our team collectively and myself individually as a leader for generations to come. Twice a year, I gather together the members of my staff team to spend time intentionally discussing a series of questions in light of our roles and responsibilities within the church staff. In asking them questions specific to their roles and responsibilities, I am honestly looking to hear others' impressions of their impact. However, I never stop there. I always turn the questions back onto myself as well. I ask them about my roles and responsibilities. I long to know their impressions of my leadership and where they see opportunities for growth or improvement. I want to know what they feel I should be letting go of, and at the same time, I want to know what they feel is so absolutely critical that I should continue pouring my time and energy into it.

By asking my staff team this series of questions twice a year, I have been able to understand and see things from a new perspective. So have they. This shared perspective has pushed us toward a deeper understanding of the mission at hand, as well as who we are in terms of meeting or missing the mark when it comes to fulfilling the mission. At times, these questions and answers are quite difficult to hear, but almost always they are fruitful in bringing about new life and hope through much-needed adaptations.

These are the questions I ask my team:

1. In terms of my ministry and role as leader, what do I need to start doing in order to become a better leader?

2. What should I stop doing as a way of creating space for new adventures?

3. What should I continue focusing on as a way of fulfilling God's mission of making disciples or building Christian community where nonreligious and nominally religious people are becoming deeply committed Christians?

(As a side note: I also share these three questions with our volunteer leadership team, who I consider to be an extension of our staff.)

QUESTION THE COMMUNITY

I ask questions of God and my staff team twice a year, but on top of that, I also dare to do the same by venturing out into the community (the mission field), engaging the people in my neighborhood with a similar set of questions. I am forever curious about what people living and working throughout the city think of our church. Do you ever wonder about that?

Almost every evening before heading to bed, I sit and reflect upon our church's perceived reputation. What did we do to impact the neighborhood today? How have we changed the world today? Oftentimes during my reflection, I wonder, *What would our neighbors say to strangers if they were asked about our church or its pastor?* This daily line of questions plagues me to the extent that twice a year (the first week of Lent and the first week of Advent), I take action. I make it a personal practice to walk through the neighborhood and engage our neighbors, both old and new, the people with almost no connection to our community. I ask them direct questions about their impressions of our ministry. This has been an invaluable practice. What I hear from our neighbors serves as a true reflection of our impact and effectiveness. In order to continue growing as leaders and communities, we must be willing to engage our mission field with questions.

Are you asking questions of your neighbors? If you have, what did they say? If you haven't, do you wonder what they might say?

Take it a step further and try to think about this as it pertains to your life as a pastor or your family as just another neighbor in the neighborhood. What would your neighbors say about you? Do they even know who you are?

These questions are critical for our ability to become Kaleidoscopic leaders, leaders who are willing to continue turning, tweaking, and adapting our approach toward becoming more like Christ by fulfilling God's mission and ministry in ways that meet people where they are and invites them to experience God's life-changing power and presence. Leaders become great not by having all the right answers, but by asking the right questions.

In Matthew 18, the disciples asked Jesus perhaps the most revealing question that plagues all leaders. They asked Jesus, "Who is the greatest in the kingdom of heaven?" (Matthew 18:1).

The disciples quite plainly wanted to know who was the best. Each one of them was hoping Jesus would say his name. Instead, Jesus turned to the crowd and called forth a child.

He sat a little child in the middle of this group of grownups, forcing them to question everything. Jesus says, "Truly I tell you, unless you change and become like children, you will never enter the kingdom of heaven" (Matthew 18:3).

To become like a child is to adopt a policy of absorbing as much as you can from the world around you. Children walk through life with wide-eyed wonder and curiosity as they see themselves as being surrounded by opportunity for growth and learning. For Matthew, becoming like a child implied becoming humble or having the ability to give up all pretensions of self-importance, independence, and self-reliance, and turning toward the God of the universe to lead. However, more importantly, becoming like a child implied that we ought to approach the world and everything in it with questions or with a posture of continual learning and adventure. The Kaleidoscopic leader's eyes should always be wide, looking for ways to draw nearer to God and to help others do the same. We should always be looking to adapt, rotate, and grow in order to uncover the good and beautiful God.

Jesus' model of leadership in ministry pushes us to never settle, but instead to keep turning until we see beautiful things. Jesus urges his disciples to keep striving, saying, "Do not let your hearts be troubled. Believe in God, believe also in me. . . . You know the way to the place where I am going" (John 14:1, 4). The way to the place where Jesus goes—the way that leads us to the kind of leaders God creates us to be and the pathway toward becoming the living body of Christ—comes through questions. Our pursuit of faith, seeking to grow in the knowledge and love of God, comes through questions—our propensity for asking questions that will push us to become better. What am I doing? What do I need to stop doing?

What must I start doing? How can I improve to better reflect the image of God to the world around me? The questioning approach to discipleship increases our leadership effectiveness throughout the generations.

Long-time, locked-in leadership at a general level elicits a worldview that would rather see the church die than change. This is what has governed our general structures from the top down for the past several decades through significant decline. Why is this? My guess is that most people are either unwilling or unable to ask the tough questions or listen to the tough answers. This cannot continue going forward. This is not Jesus' way, and it shouldn't be ours if we seek to become like Christ.

Questions for Reflection

1. How does your prayer life inform your leadership decisions?

2. What is your evaluative strategy for managing your staff team?

3. How do you actively invite feedback and professional critique?

4. Are you engaging the broader community in conversation about your church community? Who could you reach out to in order to invite feedback about the church's impact and impression?

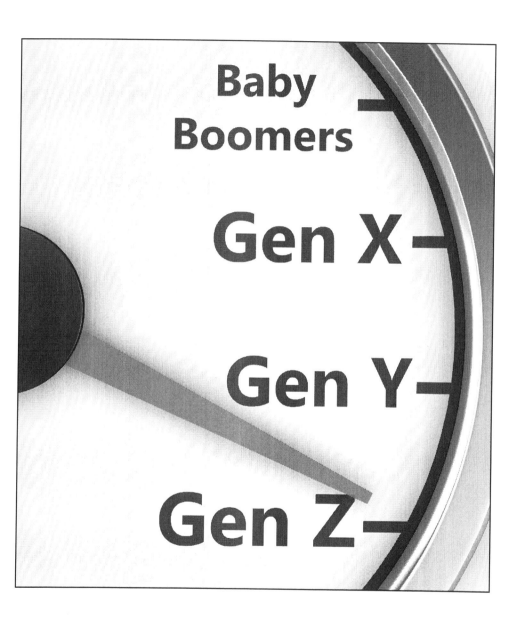

CHAPTER 7

WHAT'S POSSIBLE

The other day I had a chance to take my son to the favorite toy store in my neighborhood. As we walked into the store, I was curious as to what toy Freddy would be drawn to if I were to let him loose to run free and choose for himself. So, I put my wondering to the test. With Freddy in my arms, we entered the toy store. I walked up to the wall of toys. Every toy you might imagine was present, from stuffed animals to digital pets and monster trucks to video games. I wondered to myself, *What toy would he choose?*

He selected a jack-in-the-box. Out of all the options, Freddy found himself drawn to a little clown hiding in a box. He could have selected anything, but chose to play with the metal box instead. In a perfect world, I suppose that Freddy would have chosen a kaleidoscope, but the fact that he bypassed all the fancy, new, modern toys argued a similar case. You don't have to become something altogether different in order to invite the people around you into an experience of holy surprise and life-changing power. The church and its leaders are like this jack-in-the-box or as I have suggested throughout this book, they are like kaleidoscopes. We have been created with the specific purpose and ability to help others see the beautiful things of God.

Jesus reminded his disciples time and time again that they had been chosen. God calls and equips us for such a time as this to help others see the life-changing power of Christ. God did not make a mistake with us, though at times we might feel otherwise. Like a timeless kaleidoscope, even though we don't look as cool as the latest set of Legos or seem to have the broad functionality of the latest gaming system, God assures us that we have the capacity to reveal God's life-changing image to the world around us. We mustn't ever forget this.

As noted earlier, studies will show that the emerging generations are leaving the church faster than any generation before them. These same studies show, however, that the members of these generations are also desperate for deep, meaningful relationships. They are looking for someone to lead them to the life they're looking for. In other words, they are longing to go to the place where Jesus is going, a picture of a preferred future. What's crazy about that is Jesus assures his disciples and the church's leaders by saying that "we know the way to this place." The church is perfectly equipped and positioned to lead the generations toward the life that really is life, if only we had the courage to go and do likewise.

The very last words that Jesus offered his disciples in the Gospel of Matthew are known as the Great Commission. Jesus came and said to them, "All authority in heaven and on earth has been given to me. Go therefore and make disciples of all nations, baptizing them in the name of the Father and of the Son and of the Holy Spirit, and teaching them to obey everything that I have commanded you. And remember, I am with you always, to the end of the age" (Matthew 28:18-20).

GO THEREFORE AND MAKE DISCIPLES OF ALL NATIONS

This is our purpose. These are our marching orders. This is our end, meaning that God calls us to love God and love neighbors with the ultimate purpose of making disciples of all nations. This passage of Scripture guides my life; it excites me, and I find my heart and soul satisfied whenever I make a connection with someone to this end. Whenever I witness a personal conversion, whenever I participate in the sacrament of holy baptism, whenever we welcome new members to the life of our church or have any sort of increase in participation and involvement within the church through worship, community life, children's ministries, or missions, I find life. These moments satisfy my soul because they are indicators pointing toward fruitfulness in fulfilling the Great Commission, this foundational teaching within the life of our faith.

Have you ever noticed how little instruction Jesus offers around how we are to actually do this? Jesus' clarity about the intended audience (all nations) does not carry over into the level of detail describing how we are to actually "make disciples." Jesus never mentioned that we should pursue this mission with particular styles of preaching, singing, teaching, serving, debating, convincing, posting, grandstanding, or any other manner deemed comfortable for churches and their leaders. Jesus doesn't say anything at all about the how when it comes to fulfilling our mission. So, the question we are called to wrestle with as church leaders is a question of practice: How are we to go, therefore, and introduce people to the life-saving power of Jesus Christ?

Evangelism is a word that comes ultimately from the Ancient Greek word *euangelion,* which when translated literally means "good news" or "good message." This is the word most of the earliest disciples would have used to describe the gospel, the story of Jesus Christ's life, death, and resurrection. From this word *euangelion* comes words like "evangelism" or "evangelist."

Evangelism is the study of the practice of sharing the good news of Jesus Christ. An evangelist is nothing more than a person who is known for her or his ability to share the good story or the good news. Throughout Scripture, we see this word or one of its derivatives approximately forty-one different times, and from its use one thing becomes clear: Church leaders are called to be evangelists, to be known by our propensity for sharing the story of Jesus' life, death, and resurrection. In doing this, we will be able to fulfill the Great Commission. Telling good stories, the practice of evangelism, is the primary way God calls us to fulfill our purpose. As God's evangels or storytellers, we are called to share the story in order to invite people into the life-changing knowledge and love of God. We tell stories so that others might meet God.

John Wesley talked at length about our call to evangelism and its centrality to our life of faith. He often said that the role of a great preacher or any disciple for that matter was to live, lead, and preach with an evangelistic love of God and neighbor. Everything we did ought to tell the story of Jesus and his love for us. Our lives should share the stories of our faith and our love for God wherever we go. In fact, John Wesley went so far as to say that disciples should set ourselves on fire with the power of the Holy Spirit, meaning we should get so caught up and so enthusiastic in our faith that people from everywhere, from all ends of the earth, would come simply to watch us burn with the love of God.

He urged Christians additionally, saying, "So by all means do all the good you can, in all the places you can, to all the people you can, in every way that you can, so that people every time they meet you will have to look but once and see the light of Christ and give glory to God their Father in heaven by your good works."

Evangelism shouldn't be empty; it shouldn't be surface; it shouldn't be focused on practice and strategy or by using people as a means to an end. It should be compelling. This requires two things of us.

To be an evangelist, we must first be willing to listen to others intentionally. Secondly, we must be willing to share our own story, vulnerably and authentically in response. This, of course, would assume that you actually have a personal story of good news to share.

WHAT'S YOUR STORY?

When you have a story and you're willing to share it vulnerably, amazing things happen when you actually share it. I love the psalmist who demonstrated the courage to share his story by saying, "Come and hear, all you who fear God, and I will tell what he has done for me. I cried aloud to him, and he was extolled with my tongue. If I had cherished iniquity in my heart, the Lord would not have listened. But truly God has listened; he has given heed to the words of my prayer. Blessed be God, because he has not rejected my prayer or removed his steadfast love from me" (Psalm 66:16-20).

The psalmist boldly invited the people around him by saying, "Come all you fear, all who are shackled; come all you who are in the darkness." And then he shared his story, "For I was there once too. When I was in the darkest place, I cried out to God. I extolled God with my tongue. . . . I believed that God was treating me unfairly, and I was upset. . . . I was so angry that God should have stopped listening to me . . . but yet he didn't! Instead, he heard my cries and despite my anger, God did not reject me. His steadfast love remained with me. He loved me and promised to never let me go. Not even my anger excludes me from feasting at his table, nor will my questions or my doubt or my addiction or my whatever. . . ."

The psalmist not only shared this story, but he believed it so deeply, it impacted him so greatly that he couldn't help but sing of it, so that anyone with ears could hear it and never forget it!

What's your story? Do you have one? How has God changed your life? How are you different because of Jesus Christ?

When people ask you about faith, do you respond with answers and arguments or do you share your personal story of why Jesus matters to you? How are you different because of God? Is this evident?

In his letter to the church at Corinth, the apostle Paul writes, "We are ambassadors for Christ, since God is making his appeal through us" (2 Corinthians 5:20).

Paul says that we, our lives, what we do and say, are the primary way God makes God's appeal to the rest of the world. We are God's ambassadors, God's representatives; we are God's kaleidoscopes, carrying the capacity to share the beautiful things of God with the world around us. Churches should act similarly. We should be known by the capacity to reveal God's love.

In the Gospel of John, Jesus said that people would know we were God's by our love, by our lives, by our defining story, which is ultimately God's story. It is when we recognize that

God's story is actually our story, and this is who we are, that the good news comes through most clearly and appealingly to others.

The most impactful leaders are leaders who live a life that reveals a disposition toward the good news with every turn. They live a life that always declares there is "good news," regardless of the situation, rotation, or adaptation. What's more is that through it all, they will reject or filter all other forms of news as fake because they don't tell the whole story. In other words, all other forms of news are not worthy of sharing or reporting.

I had the chance to go and worship at a church a while ago when I was traveling. I don't often get an opportunity to worship alone, so I had high hopes that I would encounter the life-changing power of Jesus, as I don't always have this opportunity to experience worship as a parishioner. I was looking for Christ's ambassador, a leader who would have the boldness to share vulnerably about the compelling good news of Jesus. I wanted to hear a story about a God who dares to meet us in the darkness, who rescues us from the pits we find ourselves in, loosens us from the shackles of our doubt and anger, and frees us from the fear of death in order that we might find life. I wanted to hear or meet people who believed in a God who had the power to move mountains, multiply loaves and fishes, raise people from the dead, and set free all of those who are imprisoned. I wanted to have an experience of God that would change my life. Ultimately, as I sat in the sanctuary listening to the sermon, I was disappointed because I felt as though I received the same kind of information I could have just as easily found on TV through CNN or Fox News.

Jesus longs for us to make disciples of all nations, and this happens whenever we have the courage to share the compelling good news of Jesus Christ—to meet people and share with them about how our lives have been transformed by the gospel so that they might see and experience the beautiful things of God in their own lives as well. To be a kaleidoscope is to be known by the good news of Jesus Christ.

Paul writes that we are God's ambassadors. I say that we are God's kaleidoscopes—people willing to change, turn by turn, how we do things in order to better portray who God is and who we are in Christ.

Living fully into our purpose, becoming the best versions of the people we were created to be requires that we not just have a bias toward the good news through our words. We must also embody it. So, as people seeking to change the world and as people looking to share the life-changing power of Jesus Christ, I urge you to remember who you are. You are enough; God's story is your story. So, get outside the walls of the church. Break free from your comfort zone. Start working. Start talking. Start asking questions of others. Meet people where they are. Bump into people you don't already know and engage them in meaningful conversation.

Be who you are, with a newfound boldness and courage to be authentic and vulnerable, passionate and visionary, humble and relatable, always listening to the needs of others, and never forgetting that God created you, called you, and equipped you to lead uniquely for such a time as this. When we remember this and have the courage to engage the world around us, we'll have an opportunity to witness world-changing transformation and a beautiful foretaste of the kingdom of heaven here on earth.

Questions for Reflection

1. How are you known in the community? on social media?

2. How is your life different because of the life-changing grace of Jesus Christ?

3. When, where, and with whom can you share this story as a means of living into the Great Commission?

4. What must you change in order to accomplish this?

By providing relevant and affordable products and resources, real-time consulting, practical on-site, regional based training and ongoing research, Burlap helps churches of all sizes revitalize their congregations.

Burlap offers hope-based solutions to reach millennials and generation Z throughout the entire scope of its work throughout North America. We can help your church navigate the changing cultural landscape by discovering already-existing assets within your church and community to create new stories of hope and renewal.

burlap

Made in the USA
Middletown, DE
20 February 2018